CHANT-*ALL*
THE ALCHEMIST FAIRY
RETURNING
TO THE SOURCE
OF *ALL*

CHANTAL LEDUC

T0105532

CHANT-*ALL*
THE ALCHEMIST FAIRY
RETURNING
TO THE SOURCE OF *ALL*

ADAPTED AND TRANSLATED FROM THE FRENCH VERSION OF THE BOOK:
« Chantou l'Alchimiste Fée de retour à la Source » by Chantal Leduc.

"CREATED FOR YOU...
SO YOU CAN RETURN
TO THE SOURCE OF *ALL*!"

CHANTAL LEDUC,
Professional Certified NLP Coach

♠ ♥ ♦ ♣

LES ÉDITIONS CHANTOU

Balboa Press books may be ordered through booksellers or by contacting:

Balboa Press
A Division of Hay House
1663 Liberty Drive
Bloomington, IN 47403
www.balboapress.com
1-(877) 407-4847

Printed in the United States of America

ISBN: 978-1-4525-6773-0 (sc)
ISBN: 978-1-4525-6775-4 (hc)
ISBN: 978-1-4525-6774-7 (e)

Library of Congress Control Number: 2013901675

Balboa Press rev. date: 2/12/2013

I dedicate this book
to *All* the children,
t-*All* or sm-*All*,
who, one day,
felt different from *All*.

·.·´¯`·.,><((((º> <º))))><.·´¯`·.

"I am here only to be truly helpful.

I am here to represent Him Who sent me.

I do not have to worry about what to say or what

To do, because He Who sent me will direct me.

I am content to be wherever He wishes, Knowing

He goes there with me.

I will be healed as I let Him teach me to heal."

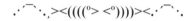

From A Course In Miracles, text.

·.·´¯`·.,><((((º> <º))))><.·´¯`·.

CONTENTS

✳ ✳ ✳

Personal Applications

Re-Sources – NON re-Sources:

- *Strong* – weak
- *Healthy* – sick
- *Confident* – fearful
- *Safe* – threatened
- *Soft* – hard
- *Tolerant* – quick-tempered
- *Non-violent* – violent
- *Thinks before acting* – acts impulsively
- *Energetic* – lazy
- *Cleaning the root chakra* – worried about survival
- *Abundantia* – filling the emptiness
- *Powerful* – powerless
- *Reconnection with Mother-Earth* – not grounded

☆ · . ، ، · ´ ⁻ ` · . ، ، · ◻ ~ ₆ °

-._- *-._-* *-._-* *-._-* *-._-* *-._-*

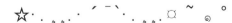

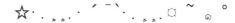
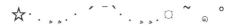

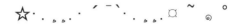

Chapter 12 – MISSION, LIFE PATH · ⌐`·.¸><((((°> <°))))><.·´⌐`·.

157

Personal Applications

Re-Sources – NON re-Sources:

- *Determined* – perplexed
- *Learn to recognize your* – "Symptoms of dizziness"
- *Flexible* – stubborn
- *Love* – Judgment, judge → lack of Love
- *Inspired by spontaneous ideas*

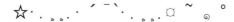

Chapter 13 – TREASURE ◕‿◕

167

Personal Applications

Re-Sources – NON re-Sources:

- *Tolerant* – im-patient, intolerant
- *Grounded* – not grounded
- *Breathing exercise...* shallow breathing
- *Perseverance, consistent* – lack of perseverance, inconsistent
- *Detachment* – attachment

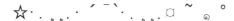

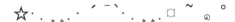

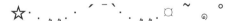

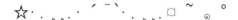

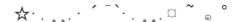

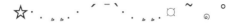

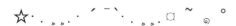

Appendix

Gratitude

‡

First, I would like to thank my Guides, God, Angels, Archangels, and *All* the Light workers who helped me achieve this beautiful dream. I would also like to thank Jesus, Mother Mary, Kwan Yin, Saint-Germain, Moses, Abundantia, the Archangels Michael, Uriel, Raphael, Haniel and Gabriel for their inspiration, Love, optimism, healing, protection and guidance...

I would like to extend my thanks to every-*ONE* who participated in the creation of this beautiful project. Thank you to those who sent great ideas through the universe and gave me the chance to substantiate them. A special thank you to Michel, my life and spiritual companion, lover, partner and friend, who supported and encouraged me and trusted in my various projects. Thank you to my parents, Nicole and Denis, who gave me their contagious joy for life and ability to work and dream. Thank you to my brother Jocelyn for being who he is, a generous, good man and also a protector. I would like to thank my grandparents and late Aunt Marie for the whispers of information and guidance you send me through dreams at night and signs during the day. Thank you to Tanya, Michel's daughter, who communicated her enthusiasm and passion to me. Thank you to Maurice Dunberry, from "l'Atelier Tire-ligne", who illustrated the cover of the book following guide lines I received mostly through dreams. I would also like to thank Nathalie Hamelin for *All* the knowledge she has shared with me and Cathleen Johnston for her revisions.

Thank you *All* for tolerating my moods while I was writing this book.

Oh, yes! There were many Moods, ups and downs. For those who have never experienced writing a book... While I was writing this book I lived two different states of being. I felt as though I were pregnant and also in therapy. Writing is a creative process, a bit like being pregnant but also THE HIGHEST FORM OF THERAPY THAT EXISTS. We can often come to terms with some problems just through writing, because it is an extremely healing and liberating exercise. Furthermore, writing enables us to pass on the en*light*enment we have received as if we were naked and sharing a great part of ourselves. Writing can give rise to many emotions and feelings. Some of our many archetypes may be revealed including Alchemist, Super Mother, Saviour, Victim, Rebel, Nature Child... Thus, people around us also experience a form of HEALING because, we are *All* linked! Yes, *All* United!

Many thanks to Life

Chant-All
(Chantou)
Chantal Hart Leduc
Chant-All He-Art Le-Duc
XOXOXO

The origins...

◈

Good *night*, Good *evening*, Good *DAY*! My nickname is Chant-*All* the alchemist-fairy. Chant-*All* is derived from «Chantou» in French... I have not always been an alchemist-fairy... but yes! In fact I have always been an alchemist-fairy, but... I didn't know I was one... Yes! In fact I have always known, but... I was not *conscious*... WOWWWWW! That's it... I was not *CONSCIOUS*... I was not *conscious* of a multitude of things in my life... Oh yes! A multitude and much, much more!

You may be wondering, "What is an alchemist-fairy?" The main goal of an alchemist-fairy on this earth is to spiritualize the material, in other words, to reveal the in-*visible* or spiritual through the material, or the visible and concrete. The fairy has angelical sight: she has the nature of an angel with a big ego while the alchemist is more down to earth or grounded. They represent different parts of me. They are the perfect balance between male and rational (the alchemist) and female and intuitive (the fairy). The purpose of the alchemist is to transform lead into GOLD. The alchemist-fairy guides her brothers and sisters toward their own purification, so they can enjoy *All* their re-Sources and shine *All* their Lights. The mystical flame, the passion, the interior jewel, the inspiration, the Divine in you, the Source, the higher Self are *All* different ways of talking about your spiritual Self, the part that we have to re-tame and re-unite to be a complete BEING. HAVING... HAVING AND BEING. BEING AND HAVING. BEING... THE VERB... GOD... FAITH... GOLD... WEALTH AND ABUNDANCE! Yes! A multitude... and much, much more!

I discovered that I had many affinities with the Soul family of the alchemist-fairies while I was reading a book written by Marie Lise Labonté "Les familles d'âmes" (translated as Soul Families) while attending my classes on Tarot cards. My teacher gave me a list of books to read and despite my research, I did not find any of them when suddenly, the book of Soul families called out to me. In no time, I had read this magnificent book. The more we evolve spiritually, the more we learn who we really are and understand, more and more, the messages the Universe is sending us. At that moment, I did not have to read the books my teacher had suggested to me only the ONE my Soul wanted me to read. That was what I allowed mySelf to do, that was *All*. In the past, I might have doubted, but not at that stage of my life. Because I am not at my first incarnation and because I like to learn it *All* (Chant-*All*), I saw mySelf in almost every Soul family that Marie Lise described. Because I am curious by nature and I want to know it *All*, I often belong in several groups at the same time. After a few moments of meditation and a lot of intuition, I quickly realized that the family that looked the most like me was the alchemist-fairy family. After *All*, a few years ago, I was an analytical chemistry technician for nearly seven years at Safety-Kleen, a company that recycles hazardous wastes. In addition, the main goal of the fairy is to protect animals and the environment... By nature, I am a great animal protector. I take care of wild birds that fail their first flight. I feed homeless cats. We even adopted a male cat that used to be homeless and called him "Bob the rectangular sponge". I feel very close to animals and nature, as though I understand them and can feel what they feel, as if we were *All* linked! Yes, *All* United!

I was born Chantal Hart in Huntingdon. Hart (He-*art*) is my father's last name. When I was 19, my parents divorced. I also divorced and decided to take my mother's last name: Leduc (Le-

Duc). At the age of 20 I was living with a new identity. Chantal Leduc was born. I was still living in Huntingdon, but my karmas changed. My energy also changed. My expression was transformed with my new identity. I became more feminine, more Yin with time. However, there had been a separation ... and "WE" had to fix it. At that time, "WE" were still un-*Conscious*. Often, to be more balanced, we must go to extremes to find our own perfect balance. I changed from a very analytical and critical personality, to a personality that loved change and became more adaptable and social, even more social than I had been before. I inherited my balance and caution from the name Hart, but I was easily influenced. By contrast, the name Leduc made me more understanding and worthy, but also excessively emotional. The only part that did not change was the ONE related to my first name. Chantal brings me my very great curiosity, dynamism, sociable nature but also ambivalence. Chantal Hart had a great need to speak and communicate. Chantal Leduc has, above *All*, a need to create and succeed with several projects. She is very original, even on the fringe. Whether she is Chantal Hart or Leduc what she produces is still the same. She fulfills. She perseveres, and she is well organized. As Chantal Hart, my karma was connected at the level of organization and work, conciliation and the couple and at the level of confidence and pessimism. As Chantal Leduc, my karmas were transformed. I no longer had any problems with organization or work, but I had emotional problems and difficulty opening up to others. I passed from inspiration and effectiveness to harmony and responsibility. My life path or my numerology remained the same because my date of birth did not change, so I am still interested in the inner life, wisdom and independence.

Along came the thirties and they came a little bit too fast for me. When I was young I thought I would not make it through the thirties. I believed that after the twenties everything was finished for me. When I made it to twenty-nine and a half, the bell rang and rang loudly. I questioned whether I was with the right person (eleven years with the same man)? Did I want to continue with the kind of job I had? Was I in the right place at the right time? I was asking the existential questions you ask when you reach the end of your thirties or forties, but not at the end of the twenties like I did. When I turned thirty I left my life companion and moved back to my mother's home. I continued to date him for five years and I became single again. I bought myself a condo. I worked two jobs at Safety-Kleen and in a restaurant, and I attended university. I was studying for a bachelor's degree in administration (financial planner) at that time, and I changed for a certificate in psychology. I wanted to understand mySelf and the relationship I had experienced with my former partner... I also registered in NLP (neuro linguistic programming) at the CQPNL (Centre Québecois Program-mation Neuro Linguistique), to become a Certified NLP Coach. Meanwhile, my gifts began to appear in my life... another important step on my path. Life helped to celebrate this great change by introducing me to someone, a new friend, who gave me the nickname: Chant-*All* (Chantou). My Soul felt a strong resonance upon hearing my new name: Chant-*All* (Chantou). I felt chills *All* over my body from head to toe. In November 2001, Chant-*All* (Chantou) was born at the age of thirty. I experienced a transformation and not a death as I had expected... Death is a transformation, a positive transformation, the end of a step and the beginning of another. The butterfly emerges from its cocoon! Re-birth...

You know, in some cultures, when a person makes a significant step or a significant change in his life, he is given a new name, a new identity. That is exactly what happened to me. Life magically ensured that I lived a change of identity, without my noticing it. From my birth to the age of 19, my name was Chantal Hart. From 19 to 30, my name was Chantal Leduc. Since the age of 30, my nickname has been Chant-*All* (Chantou) and my name is Chantal Leduc. Sometime soon I will return to the courthouse and change my name again to Chantal Hart Leduc, even though I have thought of mySelf as Chantal Hart Leduc (Chant-*All* He-*Art* Le-*Duc*) for a while. I accept *All* parts of mySelf. I love them and I live very well with them. Furthermore, I eliminate karmas with *All* these names. Ha! Ha! Now you know that my feminine part is Leduc, my masculine part is Hart, my Soul is Chant-*All* or Chantou, my uniqueness is Chantal and my Soul family is The Alchemist-fairies. If you see me somewhere, feel free to call me by my nickname "Chant-*All* or Chantou" that way you will communicate directly with my Soul something it loves. To me, Chantal sounds more individual and Chant-*All* (Chantou) more Universe-*All*. I have a Self that is Me and another that is We...US, ONE, ALL. That is the connection between you and me! I knew we were *All* linked, *All* United!

As I mentioned earlier, I am curious by nature. I am 40 years old, and I have been studying since the age of 5. Do the math by subtracting six to 12 months, and you will be very close to the number of years I have wanted to study. Wanted, yes, and I will continue to study for the rest of my life because I love to learn. Learning is crucial in my life. I am here to learn. I will share my en*light*enment and *know*ledge with you in this book and those to come, because I must re-establish the balance. For several years, I have been the one receiving and now it is my turn to give. I wrote this book through the intervention of my dreams. During my Tarot classes, I had to sleep with each card that I was studying for five nights and I had to write down my dreams in the morning. It was not a burden for me, because I had been writing down my dreams every morning for several years by then. The dreams I had during my Tarot classes, among others, inspired me to write this book. The twenty-two chapters in this book combine, in fact, *All* my various areas of *know*ledge which include tarot, numerology, NLP, angels, prayers, affirmations, meditation, Laws of the Universe, chakras, and so on. I wrote this book using the language of the Soul, the language of the He-*Art*. In other words, do not necessarily try to understand everything you read with your logical or rational mind, because this book has been designed to heal the Soul. There is no better way to communicate with the Soul than through symbols, metaphors, stories and personal applications! So, let me recount...

Chapter 1

FAITH
†

It is the beginning...

The Juggler, the Wizard, the Magician, the Alchemist... are *All* characters with huge potential. They are equipped with *All* the necessary tools. They can do *All*! The real secret is in the "Law of the WILL".

The Divinity that comes to mind when describing this image is Jesus. He came to Earth to show us that we have everything inside of us. Through his words, actions and inspiration he has shown that *All* re-Sources are within us. When he said, "I WILL that the WILL of God be done", we can feel in every inch of our being that God's WILL is to fulfill *All* our desires, especially those connected to our He-*Art*, and we can also hear that our WILLingness must be used to maintain a "clear vision" of our intention. By nourishing our desire with faith, we WILL receive what we have been asking for. On the other hand, we must not be weak. Faith is a very great Source of power and strength, because it requires a lot of WILLingness from us.

All we finally have to do is to open the door of our heart to receive the Heavenly messages predestined for us. Furthermore, when we give flight to our Spirit and Soul, we feel released, lighter and freer... By breaking down the walls around our heart, we hear our inner voice... our intuition... our wisdom. God is our center. This is our wealth! To illustrate this, in the book *A Course in Miracles*, it is written: "Christ is in me, and where He is God must be, for Christ is part of Him." This affirmation reinforces the idea that we have *All* the potential in us to create *All* we desire. However, we must be careful what we wish for!

This brings me to tell you that we are co-creators of our lives. We are working in concert with God to create our own existence, the very ONE we have imagined. We participate with God in making our lives what they are. We have a lot of power, but are we really *conscious*? Do we really know? We have a lot of power, because what we think, say or do, WILL come together sooner or later on our path. Our thoughts, words, writings, and actions are *All*... forms of requests. "Ask and ye shall receive" said Christ. Thus, our thoughts, words, actions and writings are like many forms of prayer... Oops! The *conscience* is becoming involved.

We must be *aware* of what we think, say, do and write... because it will come back to us. "Give and you'll receive" said the Saviour. That is how we participate in creation. It is up to us to be careful what energy we send into the Universe. Here is a situation that I experienced recently. On a beautiful afternoon, I decided to go to the jeweller. I wanted to park my car in front of the store. At the last minute I saw a parking spot, but until I was parked, I blocked the traffic behind me. A lady in a van behind me was angry and I saw her talking loudly and making gestures. I guess I was not very Zen that day, because I said a few bad words in my head at that moment. As I finally finished parking the car, the lady in the van passed by and her passenger said the same bad words I had just thought seconds before. I howled with laughter! I got as good as I gave. As we become increasingly *aware*, life quickly shows us what we have created, especially when it comes to thoughts, words or behaviours that are not entirely centered on

Love. At that moment, we are creating what we call karma. When we judge or criticize, we are also judged or criticized. When we hate or convict, we are also hated or convicted and so on, until we understand. The karmas are lessons that we have come here to resolve in our human experience. *Awakening* will begin at the required moment, if applicable. Ill effects and dis-*ease*s are often the result of our creations or imagination taking the wrong path... a non *Luminous* ONE. Because of those negative creations, we obtain results that express non *harmonious* insights. The body then creates ill effects and dis-*ease* which are messages sent to help us understand that there is something wrong in our life. Sometimes you have to experience the dis-*ease* itself or perhaps you are a healer and you need to experience it before you can help others, although not necessarily. Our body talks to us *All* the time and we just have to listen. Jesus knew that the dis-*ease*s were often the result of our thoughts, words and behaviour... dis-*oriented* on Love. After curing a patient, he said: «Go and sin no more, lest a worse thing come him. » Now, we know sin is the opposite of joy so have faith and be happy!

I am guided to help people *awaken*, so their Souls may vibe in harmony as they are intended to. I consider mySelf a "Soul *Awakener*". I receive Celestial messages for the evolution of my clients. I connect with their Souls and relay messages from them. My life path is to help my brothers and sisters harmonize their being on Earth... Body-Spirit-Soul the Holy Trinity! What? The idea is to be a complete being from within. The ultimate goal is to be able to satisfy our needs and improve our happiness without requiring anything from the outside world.

When there is a non *harmonious* inner Self (or outer Self, because both are the same), it is because the physical body is not aligned with the Soul. Our feelings are confused, as though something was missing, and with time illness is created. The Soul lives in deep sorrow; because God's Divine purpose is not fulfilled. You know the life path YOU HAVE CHOSEN to Light up your life. Your Soul knows your Divine plan and knows when you are doing something other than what you were born for, which explains why you feel the urgent need to do the things you feel so deeply. As if we must hurry to act without knowing exactly what it is we have to do. We may not know what to do, but at least we are *conscious* and feel that we have to accomplish something, and that time is running out.

When we are in total *harmony*, we feel a great joy, almost indescribable, as if we were bubbles in a luxurious bottle of champagne not a "Cordon Rouge", but high class champagne. People see us and smile as though they see or hear our inner laugh, because we are the same inside and out. We attract abundance, prosperity, joy and Love because we are happy and in *harmony* with *All* parts of ourselves. As I mentioned earlier, I am a "Soul *Awakener*", but occasionally it still happens that I am not in total *harmony* with my own Soul. That is perfectly normal, because I was dis-*connected* from it for a large part of my life. Consequently, sometimes I take a wrong path and return to my old habits. When that happens, life tells me quickly enough. Abundance decreases, the phone rings less, my intuition does not respond and ideas do not come easily... I sense that I cannot teach or give what I do not have mySelf, just like the old saying, "How can you Love someone else if you don't Love yourSelf?" How can I help someone to vibrate harmoniously with his Soul if I am in rebellion with mine and what it tells me to do? Anyway, do not worry, your guides, intuition, inner voice and Christ within you or your higher Self will tell you who to call when you need it the most and at the right moment for you. BE patient. Nothing occurs by pure coincidence. Everything happens for a reason. So, we have everything inside us to accomplish what we REALLY desire, *All* we need is faith and a bit of patience, and the trick is done (*All* WILL be well). If you still cannot believe it, I will ask you to close your eyes and imagine I have a beautiful magic wand, and POOF! I will cast a spell on you and from now on you can do everything you wish! Yes, everything is inside you... Yes, absolutely everything!

Personal Applications

This chapter discusses the work as it relates to the evolution of an individual's personality. The type of person we are looking at is totally un-*conscious* of her own power and strength and does not even know that she is the creator of her own existence. In-*stability* may be present in her world: fear and weakness may also be present. This could be a person who is not anchored or grounded to our dear Mother-Earth. There may be a lack of confidence and faith, causing in-*security*. We could also be dealing with in-*activity*, stagnation, laziness... if and of course only if, there are emotional blockages. Otherwise, someone who vibrates in a vortex of positive energy will resonate with the total power, strength and courage she is supposed to have. This person possesses a masculine energy and is very active thanks to a complete absence of need and fear. She will express no signs of violence or anger. She knows her strength. She knows what she has. She is acting with *All* her strength and power.

To determine if there is emotional blockage in your personal life, I suggest you take the time to answer the following questions as honestly as possible:

✓ **Do you consider yourSelf a weak person?**

If so, under what circumstances do you experience weakness?

How do you know?

Are there occasions when you feel *strong*?

What re-Sources are missing in your present life that would make you *stronger*?

How would you know that you are *strong*, or that you have *strength*? What do you see? What do you hear? What do you feel? Insert everything you see, hear and feel into *All* the cells of your being... and feel the *strength* in you. Then memorize this experience and give it a name, an image, a colour, or a flavour... Make sure that you have access to it whenever you want in the future. Put it in a safe place inside you...

✓ **Are you often sick?**

If so, consider the situations that can or may make you sick. Identify them.

How can you be certain that these kinds of situations can make you sick?

What can you do to improve the situation and make yourSelf *healthy* again?

If you do not know, pretend you know... You must know someone who is *healthy*, so think about what exactly that person does to be *healthy*? Now, what can you do to be *healthier*?

Have there been any events in your life that have had favourable effects on your *health*?

What could you do in your present life to increase the number of occasions that would have beneficial effects on your *health*? What are you waiting for?

✓ **Are you a fearful person?**

If so, when do you experience a sense of fear?

Are there occasions in your life when you have felt *confident*?

Look at your experiences of total *confidence* and see how they differ from your experiences of fear. What have you found? Consider the following chart and then create your own:

Experience of *confidence*	Experience of fear
I feel good about myself.	I don't feel good about myself.
I experience a sense of peace, love and joy.	I feel upset. I am nervous and anxious.
I glow. I am inspired. I feel positive energy.	I am in a dark mood. I have negative thoughts.

✓ **Do you often feel threatened?**

If so, under what circumstances do you feel threatened?

Are there occasions in your life in which you have felt completely *secure*?

What do you think is missing in your present life that would make you feel *safe*? Why?

What can you do, right here and now, to bring those missing items into your life?

✓ **Are you a hard person?**

If so, I recommend that you meditate on the subject. Find a comfortable position and ask to be en*light*ened about why you are a hard person... I suggest you take the time to understand what there is to understand specifically at this level. Then, I would ask you to write down what you have received. This contemplation could take several days, even weeks. Write down what you receive each day and meditate on it... Do this exercise for as long as you feel you need to.

✓ **Are you quick-tempered?**

If so why?

When are you the most likely to be angry? Why?

How can you bring more *tolerance* into your life, right here and now?

Where do you think this anger comes from?

Try to return to the Source of this anger and bring *gentleness* into your life now. Close your eyes and return to the Source of the emotion. Trust yourSelf; you will naturally go back by simply sending out the intention... Then give it a new Source, a *softer* ONE. This Source of *gentleness* may be whatever you want. Give it a *soft* colour... a *sweet* smell... a *sweet* sound... a *sweet* name... see it... hear it... feel it... You could ask for help from Angels, Archangels, Ascended Masters, your Guides, God... as you wish. Stay there as long as you desire simply feeling that *gentleness* inside you... When you are ready, open your eyes. From now on, every time you feel anger, reorient yourSelf by fully recalling this experience of *gentleness*. Bring the emotion straight to your heart and enclose it with LOVE. Repeat the exercise every time the emotion of anger returns and, with time, the anger will totally disappear. Being ever more *aware* and *conscious* is the key to healing yourSelf!

✓ **Do you tend to be violent?**

Why do you think you are violent?

What lies behind this behaviour or that emotion?

Can you do something else to express this violence without hurting anyone in any way? For example through the arts, physical exercise, writing...

Have you ever been through an experience in your life in which you responded without violence?

How can you be less violent *(pacifism)* right here and now?

A warrior often tends to be violent, yet violence breeds violence in return. The idea is to use that energy effectively. It is a very powerful energy and you must find a way to release it. You must express it, but without harming anyone. I advise you not to keep this type of emotion inside you. Express it through singing or writing, either by doing a sport, martial art or kickboxing, for example, but you must channel this energy out of your body. Describe to me how are you going to proceed?

✓ **Do you tend to act without thinking?**

Are you someone who acts first and thinks later?

If so, under what circumstances do you act without *thinking*?

Are there occasions in your life when you do *think before acting*?

Remember an experience when you did *think before acting*. Take note of that moment. Take a look at the image of this moment, as if it was a picture. What do you see? What do you feel? What do you hear? What do you smell? Do you have a particular taste in your mouth?

Now, do the same thing, but memorize an experience when you have acted without thinking. Take note of that moment. Look at the image of this moment as if it was a picture. What do you see? What do you feel? What do you hear? What do you smell? Do you have a particular taste in your mouth?

Compare the two experiences and notice the differences. In the future, when you act blindly or without thinking, you will notice it immediately and you will be able to correct it, because you now know the characteristics.

✓ **Are you lazy?**

If so, why do you define yourSelf as a lazy person?

Are there days when you feel you are not a lazy person?

Why do you think you are more *energetic* some days and not others?

Remember a day when you were *energetic*. Feel the emotion, the *energy* you experienced at that precise moment. Stay in that state, and say aloud: "I am an *energetic* person, right here, right now and forever!" Write this affirmation on a piece of paper, stick it on your bathroom mirror and repeat it as often as possible every day.

✓ **Are you worried in general about your survival?**

If so, what do you think you need to survive?

What are you lacking?

Sometimes people who have an emotional blockage at the level of the first chakra, the root chakra, fear for their survival. This chakra represents survival, instincts, security and the basics of life. When there is an emotional blockage at this level, depending on the person or the situation, the chakra may choke up, turn in the wrong direction (counter clockwise), reduce or increase its frequency and get smaller or bigger. Visualize it like a ceiling fan or a funnel, for example, at the base of your spine, the coccyx. The shade you should see it as is a bright reddish colour, but any colour you see it is the right one.... It turns clockwise. You can clean it under the shower by putting your left hand on it and unwinding it with your right hand, your fingers pointing towards your body. Turn three times counterclockwise and put your hand under the water a few seconds, then unwind it three times but clockwise this time. Do this exercise for as many days you feel you need to. With time, you will probably feel it in your own body.

✓ Is there anything missing in your life?

How do you know there is something missing in your life?

Do you believe lack REALLY exists?

What do you think you are missing?

Has it ever happened that you thought you would lack something in the future?

Are you aware that you have probably programmed that lack yourSelf?

Abundance exists so that we can *All* enjoy it. Because the game of life is: "Ask and you shall receive", I suggest that you pay attention to what you are asking for in general. If you feel there is something missing in your life, you must necessarily ask for it. By asking, I mean asking in *All* the possible ways: through words, thoughts, actions, emotions... If you are not receiving LOVE in your life, it is probably because you are not giving any to others or yourSelf. Do you understand? If, for example, you have been afraid that you might run out of money, food, or anything else, and you have put some aside EXCESSIVELY, do not be surprised if you run out one of these days. I suggest you take a few minutes to meditate and be *aware* of *All* the feelings you have related to the fact you might run out of something in the future. Simply ask to be informed about the Source of these feelings and you will receive a response eventually. However, be careful, the answer may take several possible forms. It is up to you to interpret the messages you receive! (And this is something I can help you with.)

"Abundantia is a beautiful goddess of success, prosperity, abundance and good fortune, she is also considered to be a protector of savings, investments and wealth", according to the writings of Doreen Virtue in her book *Archangels & Ascended Masters*. If you believe in goddesses, I suggest you call upon Abundantia by saying a beautiful prayer, because her mission is to show us the way to "the Source of *All*". However, we must ask her first. Personally, I pray every day and almost every time I thank Abundantia for the abundance in my life!

P.S.:　By prayer, I am not referring to religious prayers, but specifically to the words that you receive intuitively when you go to pray. Let yourSelf be guided by the wisdom or your He-*Art*...

✓ **Do you consider yourSelf a coward?**

If so, when do you think you are the most cowardly?

Have you ever had an experience where you felt you had *power*?

If so, make a note of that experience. If not, you must certainly know someone who has experienced great *power*. It might be a friend, a famous person, a person out of history perhaps, or anyone else. Try to feel the experience of *power* in *All* your being... Give it a colour... a smell... an image... a name... Pretend you are living the experience, here and now. Take *All* the time you need to really see, hear, feel and taste this beautiful experience of complete

POWER. Now, take *All* the goodness of this wonderful experience of *power* with you as best you can, so you have access to the *POWER* whenever you want in the future. Now you can access this great *POWER* anytime you wish. It will always be a part of you... Relive an experience of cowardice and as soon as you feel the emotion, bring back the energy from the experience of *POWER* immediately. Take the time to enjoy the experience of great *POWER*... Imagine another experience of cowardice that could take place in the future. As soon as you feel the emotion of cowardice, bring back the energy of your experience of *POWER* immediately. Take the time to savour this great experience of *POWER*... Repeat this exercise until you cannot feel the emotion of cowardice anymore... You are a perfect, fully *powerful* being... here, now and forever!

✓ **Do you feel that you are not *connected* to Mother-Earth? There are several reasons why many of us are not grounded; here are some examples:**

Did you have relationship problems with your biological or adoptive mother? Did you ever feel that your mother was absent?

Have you ever felt as if you were a butterfly?

Have you ever had any problems with your legs, knees or feet?

Have you ever had an accident? A car accident or any other kind?

Do you move often?

Do you travel by plane a lot?

Has anyone ever been physically, sexually or verbally aggressive towards you?

If you answered yes to one of these questions, then it is very possible you are not *connected* to Mother-Earth. I suggest you do the following exercise once a day, preferably in the morning when you wake up:

Sit down and visualize roots growing from the soles of your feet and moving towards the center of the Earth. Feel the heat, safety, security, Abundance, creativity and Love of Mother-Earth passing through the roots and going directly into your feet. You will feel the energy flowing through your feet. You will then feel *All* of this beautiful energy in your knees, legs, buttocks, waist, stomach, chest, shoulders, arms, hands, neck, head, in *All* your organs in *All* your body and in *All* the cells of your being. You are now filled with the heat, safety, security, Abundance, creativity and LOVE of Mother-Earth.

Chapter 2

Spirituality
✻

I was walking on my life path with several wounds to the Soul. Wounds I have been carrying around with me for several lives now. Deep wounds that are as deep as the depths of the seas. Black seas, red seas... Black feelings, red passion... Blue emotion or communication... Feeling... rejection... feelings a long time un-*forgiven*, un-*spoken*... I saw the wounds to my Soul in my dreams at night as wounds on my heels. In some cultures, there are those who believe that the Soul comes out of the body by way of the heel when it dies or... rises.

We receive ideas at night. At night we are informed, purified, cured and protected. I travel at night under the Light of the moon and bring images and symbols of the un-*conscious* back with me to the surface. At night, I go into the depths of un-*conscious*-ness to discover the reason why I have lived this or that emotion during the day. In the morning, I realize, or rather, I *awaken*.

I have a little secret I want to share with you: my discoveries, I simply ask for them, but Shh! don't tell anybody, this is a secret. I do not know why, yes, I do know. It is because I receive the information I need or the answers to my questions. I ask mySelf a question, and there is the answer! The answer may come in many ways, through someone else, or a book, or an intuition... It almost seems like magic. If I believed in magic, I would say it is magic, but it isn't, is it?

In chapter 1, we saw that, through imagination, words and thoughts, we create our own reality in *All conscious*-ness I hope. Now, we will see that there are various ways to receive information, re-Sources, solutions, *know*ledge or cures. It could be in our sleep at night, through prayer, meditation, singing, chanting... Use the technique that resonates most in you, the one you feel the strongest and is the easiest for you. The goal is to stop mental activity and empty your mind. Everything can be found in emptiness. Emptiness gives us the power to redirect our thoughts, allowing us to create and receive positive thoughts, thoughts that are centered on Love. Love is the key to everything. Love opens doors that have been closed for many years, even several lives. Love cures *All*!

Life is a game. Jesus Christ has shown us that we only have to give and we will receive. Of course, we receive what we have given and even more. For example, when we launch a boomerang what we send has energy in the Universe and we shall receive it back with almost the same energy. In contrast, think of *All* the many wars, battles, conflicts, separations that create so much negative energy, dis-*harmony*, im-*balance*, aches, dis-*eases*, and yet are considered totally normal; normal for whom? Normal, perhaps, for people who are asleep and are not *conscious*. When will we finally *wake* up and live in *harmony*? Live in *harmony* first with our Soul. Live in *harmony* first with ourselves, and after, and only after, with others... The illness that exists on our planet is the fact that we consider it NORMAL for life to be a battle, instead of allowing life's truth, beauty, joy and Love to surround us. Excuse me, I am making this up, we have created an eternal battle, so how can we receive or simply see LOVE, and how can we feel joy? Life is a game, as Florence Scovel Shinn says in her book *The Game of Life*, "it is a game, however, which cannot be played successfully without the knowledge of spiritual law". I believe we must rise to the level of Spiritual Laws by applying them the best we can and *voila*! Simple is it not? This brings me to the second spiritual law: "The Law of Attraction". I want you to savour, here and now, the energy of this Law because it allows us to know everything. As I mentioned earlier, the trick is to control your mental state. This way you become a channel, ask, and you will receive. It is another beautiful reason to have beautiful thoughts, say nice words, act to the best of our ability, and much, much more... After *All*, we are created by God, our father.

In other words, this Law enables us to know everything. We already know everything. Everything is inside us. Yes, everything is in us. All our re-Sources are inside us. That is why, by meditating, for example, we re-*connect* to our Soul, our intuition, our inner voice, our guide, our higher Self... Intuition teaches us from the inner Self.

Meditating allows us to control our minds which can sometimes be out of control. The ultimate goal is to stop or to be able to stop this little hamster that is continuously running in our head... Meditation helps us to receive, hear, see, understand, feel, smell and taste something other than what we are used to... and much, much more! The ability to "Embrace Silence", as Wayne Dyer says, provides a tremendous wellness. Where we always believed we had control, we suddenly see that, in the end, we never had it at *All*. Meditation, prayer, mantras, affirmations, singing... *All* these activities enable us to stop our thoughts from continuously running away on us and take us towards what we wish for. The goal is to finally become master of our own being. The idea is to be free and in control of our life. Always remember, we are co-creators of our own existence!

Our Ego, our mind, can sometimes believe it is the master of our being and try to take control, which is precisely what should not happen. The Ego creates a lot of negative thoughts, feelings of guilt, deprecation, dis-*ease*, pain, loneliness, rejection and feelings of separateness. It becomes an entity of its own. Your goal is to heal. The recovery first consists of being *aware* of your various wounds and to be *conscious* of your conflicts, (remember, the inner Self is the same as the outer Self), and then being *aware* of the role your Ego plays in your life. Only, when you feel that your Ego is less awkward, will you be able to be guided by an interior force. With time and practice, you will get some surprising results. How will you know when your Ego is less in the way? Well, I will ask you to IDENTIFY your Ego first. I am, personally, very often informed through my dreams. I know the symbol that represents my Ego, in fact, it is a person. In the beginning, she (the person) was very often in my dreams and she had a lot of control over me, just like the Ego in everyday life. Now in my dreams, we get along fine and I do not see her anymore. I know she is there, but I don't see her in the flesh and blood. Consequently, I know she does not take up as much space as before in my life. One time, my Ego took up so much space that I became dizzy. I literally saw mySelf become angry at it, and felt physically ill, nauseated and deeply im-*balanced*. On the other hand, how could I expect to receive anything good when I had created the harm *All* by mySelf? I was angry at my Ego. I had to re-*focus* on Love and joy and in a few seconds the unrest was gone. I am *aware*, because often, when people around me are talking, I can see particles coming out of their mouths. The particles are white if they are speaking in a positive way and black if what they are saying is negative. I have had the opportunity of seeing this in a painting at an art gallery in Puerto Rico. When I saw it, I said to mySelf: "At least there is someone else who sees the same things I do. Thank God, there are at least two of us!"

I meditate, pray and sing "OM" ("OM" is a spiritual sound that opens the third eye and elevates our vibration) every day. That is how I became a channel. Excuse me; I re-became a channel because I receive a lot of information for mySelf and others too. Now, I always try to listen to my intuition and try not to resist because in every case it is right. Why, then, spend so much energy un-*necessarily*? I would like to pause here to tell you that I have a slightly rebellious side. Yes, one of my archetypes is the rebel, so in terms of rules... I even have trouble with my periods (in French menstrual period = règles; règles = rules in English); you know, the periods that women have every month? Is it because of the rules, the periods or the femininity? *All* go in the same direction, rules of my intuition...

I expanded my gifts using several techniques, but it was my training in NLP that helped me the most to recognize my abilities and talents. Everything really started at that time because I was in a favourable environment and everything was flowing in such a way that I was made *aware* of it. Was this not a happy coincidence? I remember one morning, I was on my way to the CQPNL, taking the Mercier Bridge to get there, but I never made it to school and I knew beforehand that I would not. Something inside of me told me that the car was going to breakdown. I remember wondering if I could miss a day and just as I decided it would be okay, smoke started coming out of the hood. I headed toward the exit I felt I had to take and there, within a few yards, was a gas station. Wow! I was stunned. I knew. I heard. I saw. After, by practicing self-hypnosis and analysing my dreams, I continued to develop my gifts. I still develop them today and my goal is to continue to do so for *All* eternity. Thanks to hypnosis, I have learned how to go into a "trance" easily, and *All* by mySelf. Now, in 2013, I can *connect* my Soul to the Souls of other people and I am able to feel their feelings, illnesses, emotions and so on in my own body. I see certain things related to them and I know what I need to know about the person, at that precise moment. I *connect* to your Soul to tell you what it has wanted to say to you for so long. It has been with you longer than your body has been; it knows why you have been incarnated here and now. In 2007, I started to write down my dreams every morning and at that time, I dreamed that I could recognize other people's illnesses. I have dreamed that I was writing books in channelling and, through automatic writing; I have dreamed that I communicated with Spirits. Dreams are like imagination, they are a form of "Clairvoyance" -Clear Seeing. They are images, symbols and symbols are exactly the language of the Soul. That is why we mediums often receive symbols as messages that we must then successfully interpret for the person they are addressed to. As you can see, everything is profoundly linked deep down. Even you and I and others are linked which is why it is so important to heal and evolve.

Personnel Applications

The subject of this chapter is related to resonance of a social matter, because we are talking about the High Priestess, the Female Pope. She appears to be a person whose life does not flow with joy, desire and pleasure; the type of person who does not know how to stop her mind for a few moments. Darkness may be present because there is no passion. Lack of vitality and competence along with shame, frustration and jealousy may sail on these waters. They are dark, troubled waters. Pleasures and needs are located in the stomach. This could be a person who has suffered aggression in the past, or has a lot of difficulty being creative, or may have experienced some sexual problems. Her femininity has perhaps been crushed or not accepted at *All*... if and of course only if, there are emotional blockages. Otherwise, anyone who vibrates in a vortex of positive energy will resonate Love of life, desire and pleasure. Because of feminine energy, this person is very sexual, passionate and also has a wilder side. She will not express any signs of shame, frustration or jealousy. She knows that she possesses a pure love of life. She acts with great passion, and her beautiful sensuality evolves in joy and beauty... She is a Mother jaguar or Great serpent from the West coast to the South. This type of person is the archetype of the lively adventurer who is pleasant, yet mysterious and secretive!

To determine if there is emotional blockage in your personal life, I suggest you take the time to answer the following questions honestly:

✓ **Are you lacking *joy* in your life?**

   If so, when does your life lack *joy*?

   What can you do to bring more *joy* into your life?

Is there anything you could do to improve your situation?

What makes you *happy*? Give at least three examples.

Take these three examples and think about how you could bring more *joy* into your life every day. The goal here is to experience *joy* to its fullest each day and then the Universe will help with the rest. On the other hand, your purpose is to be *joyful*...

Personally, I am *happy* when I sing and cook, and also when I am being creative, dancing, eating good food, learning, traveling, enjoying nature, decorating, reading and when I am in good company, and when I write too. I understand that I have to be *joyful* first, and then the rest will come. Nourishing mySelf is as important, if not more so, as taking care of others and because my nourishment brings me *joy*, so through my *joy*, I feed others. Smile and you shall receive...

✓ **What do you *desire*?**

Are they good *desires*?

For example, are you someone who might have *desires* for vengeance?

Are your *desires ones* that allow you to go forward?

If not, why do you keep them in your life?

What would happen if you suddenly let them go?

How would you feel after releasing them? What do you see? What do you hear?

You might have to leave behind people or things that harm your present evolution, which might bring chaos into your life. However, do we not say that it is through chaos that the Universe was created? In NLP, they say "Chaos brings *joy*"! So, let's be *happy*!

✓ **Do you have *fun* in life?**

If not are you perhaps too wise?

Why are you so wise?

What could you do to reach a perfect balance between wisdom and *pleasure*?

Is it not possible to be wise and have *fun* at the same time?

Please close your eyes and let wisdom flow through you. Give it a colour... smell... flavour... name... symbol... sound... Ask it to be a part of your life, now and forever, but in perfect balance... Stay in that state of union with your own wisdom for a few moments... Now, add to it an appropriate amount of *pleasure*, knowing that, in the future, this amount will be balanced in a natural way to suit the situation, and then, using your own wisdom, grant it a colour... smell... flavour... name... symbol... sound... Ask it to be a part of your life, now and forever, in perfect balance... Now, you can open your eyes knowing you have inside you the perfect recipe for wisdom with an appropriate dose of *pleasure*!

✓ **Do you live according to your *passions*?**

What brings out your *passion*?

What makes you *passionate*?

What were your *passions* when you were younger?

Make a list of *All* your *passions*, present and past. And then, on the list, check off each *passion* you have satisfied over the last month. Now draw another column and check off each one you have satisfied over the last week. Finally, draw a third column and check off those you satisfy every day. Take the time to look at the list. The more you satisfy your *passions* the more you are on the right path. Based on your list, how is your life path?

Example:

My *passions*	Satisfied during the last month	Satisfied over the last week	Satisfied every day
singing	✓	✓	✓
drawing			
painting	✓	✓	
reading	✓	✓	✓
writing	✓	✓	✓
cooking	✓	✓	✓
traveling	✓	✓	
studying	✓	✓	✓

The goal of this *consciousness* exercise is for you to take note of your *passions*, see if you satisfy them regularly or not and thus, ensure you experience them as much as possible. The closer you are to your *passions* the more wonderful you are, because you are uniting *pleasure* and *joy* in your life. Now, it is up to you to bring *passion* back into your daily life!

✓ **Do you feel ashamed?**

If so, what are you ashamed of?

Often, what we are ashamed of outside of ourselves is also inside and vice versa. For example, if you are ashamed of your mother, you are probably ashamed of a feminine part of yourSelf, since your mother symbolizes your feminine side. You may be ashamed of a part of your body, for example. What you need to know is that as long as you do not accept that part of yourSelf it will always appear as it is. The message to understand here is that if you cannot *see with the eyes of your heart*, what you do see is perceived as you perceive it! This is not reality! It is simply your own reality! Remember, the outer Self is the inner Self and vice versa. Furthermore, you can only see what you are... what you know... what you live...

✓ **Are you easily frustrated over everything and nothing?**

If so, when are you most frustrated? Why?

What could you do to behave like a *convivial person* from now on?

You have no idea? You must certainly know a *convivial person*. How does that person behave? Write a precise description of that person. In your opinion, why is that person like that and how are you different? How can you become a *convivial person*, like that person, right here and now?

Now, I would ask you to sit down and imagine that the *convivial person* is sitting nearby. Visualize that person. Feel his or her aura. Communicate with that person so that you can even smell him or her. Now, change places. Sit down at his or her place and imagine you are that person. You become the *convivial person*. You see yourSelf sitting there... You take on the *convivial person's* energy. You communicate with yourSelf sitting over there... You have the odour of the *convivial person*... You see, feel and hear just like the *convivial person*... Write what you are experiencing or say it aloud... Then, go back to your own initial position and look at what you have written or write down what you have shared aloud. Now you know what you can do to behave like a *convivial person*, every day!

✓ **Are you a jealous or envious person?**

If so when are you jealous or envious?

What can you do to be more *detached*?

I suggest you do the following liberation exercise: "take a bath to which you add a bit of sea salt. Light a candle, orange coloured if possible and Light some sage which you let burn to purify and clean the energy in the room. Lie down in the bath so that the level of the water covers your stomach. Then, ask the Archangel Michael to help you liberate yourSelf from the jealousy within you. Say a prayer, say you do not want to live with that feeling anymore in your life and that you want to be in full control of your own life, here and now. Ask that *All* feelings of jealousy near or far, be erased from your life. The Archangel Michael will cut the cord that was connecting you to jealousy. Meanwhile, visualize your sacred Chakra (located 3.5 inches above the base of the spine and orange coloured), turning three times counter clockwise, then three times clockwise". Repeat these steps three times. Then, thank him. Wash yourSelf. Then, ask Mother-Earth to remove *All* traces of purification when emptying the bath tub. Thank Mother-Earth and *All* Light beings present. You may repeat this exercise as often as you want. A minimum of three days in a row is highly recommended.

You can use the magic of stones to heal your problems at the level of the sacred Chakra. In the book: "Dictionnaire De La Lithothérapie", by Reynald Georges, on page 369, the main stones that you can apply without risks are:

Orange coloured Amber	Enstatite	Orange coloured Topaz
Orange Calcite	Hessonite Garnet	Vanadinite
Orange coloured Citrine	Spessartite Garnet	Orange coloured Zincite
Cornelian	Fire Opal	Orange Zircon
Crocoite	Sunstone	
Copper	Sphalerite	

Rhodonite is a pink stone with small black cloud-like shapes in it. It is excellent to help regulate blood flow. If you have menstrual problems, I advise you to use it. Place the stone in your underwear, for example, on your stomach at the level of your internal reproductive organs where blood clots may occur and create pain. This is also the stone to use if you have to protect yourSelf from jealousy, exaggerated Love, stubbornness and aggression. If you are under the yoke of a jealous partner, or if you are experiencing or have experienced aggression, or if your partner has been unfaithful, I suggest you make use of this beautiful stone. It has been proven to work in the past! Believe me! It can also be placed in your underwear on your stomach at the level of your internal reproductive organs to help you release fallout from your past...

N.B.: You must clean the stones before using them. Some stones can be cleaned with distilled water only, others with distilled water and salt. I suggest you simply expose them to sun and moon Light, outside if possible, for at least 24 hours, as they would be in nature, and you will be *All* set.

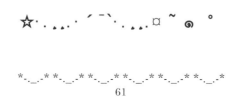

Chapter 3

COMMUNICATION
♫♪

I create and COMMUNICATE in cooperation with my feminine side. My creativity arises in solitude. A part of me is ashamed that I use my feminine side so often to communicate and create. It is daytime, we can feel the heat of the sun on our skin. I am *conscious* of my feelings... some of my feelings at least!

I create and communicate in cooperation with a Divine Strength and Power. I have frequently fraternized with my dark side. Now, I am working more often with the Luminous part, with Light Spirits, Archangels, Angels, Masters, Deities, God. One of my Guides is Jesus... It is night time and the moon is illuminated by the Sun. I am un-*conscious* that I am being guided, strongly advised and taken care of by a Divine energy at *All* times!

In my dreams at night, I see mySelf working in restaurants in this life and in other lives too (I see my past lives through dreams and flashes I receive during the day while meditating or through Self-hypnosis). The restaurant is a symbol that represents LOVE for me and *All* forms of nourishment: spiritual, intellectual, emotional... Sometimes I am the owner of the restaurant and other times, I am simply a waitress. Therefore, I am LOVE. I am a waitress of LOVE. I am a Light worker as explained by Doreen Virtue in her book: *The Light worker's way*... and I have been for a long time, quite a long time, un-*conscious* of it...

Whether or not we want it, we tend to be attracted towards what we are. However, before being able to see certain things, we must first want it or believe it. Nocturnal dreams allow us to see things locked in our un-*conscious*, sub-*conscious*. Dreams at night allow us to believe things that we do not necessarily see in the daytime. Dreams at night allow us to see... the in-*visible*. Thanks to our dreams we make the in-*visible visible*.

To create and communicate, I use *All* my intuition. Before, I was communicating much more with my masculine side. Events throughout my life occurred precisely so that I could expand my feminine abilities. For a long time, I would say, I had a masculine energy. My energy was more Yang than Yin. I had a greater affinity with boys than girls. I had a lot of "boy" friends and fewer "girl" friends, because my energy was more masculine and because I had several wounds from my experiences with my "girl" friends. In a way, I felt safer with "boys" than "girls". For such changes to occur in my life, I had to make several realizations and undergo a lot of purification. I would say that the past decade has been devoted to cleaning, awareness, purification, healing, understanding, recognition... and so on. In Feng Shui, the room in the house located on the East side reveals what we do for our health and ours is the laundry room, which is a good illustration of the cleanup I have been doing and am still doing! That is why I consider mySelf a completely different woman than I was ten or even twenty years ago.

In my dreams at night, my sub-*conscious* uses the symbol of the boat to emphasize the fact that there will be a transformation in me, some changes in my inner life, and/or also of various projects. Very often, traveling on water in dreams indicates great transformation in our life. The symbols that appear to me at night in dreams are no different, in terms of their interpretation, from those that appear in the daytime. What happens then with the people who suffer from sea sickness? Yes, I agree that these people are afraid of losing control with their travel sickness, but they are also afraid of transformations, changes and newness in their lives. This is because transformations or changes often come when we do not have any control. Moreover, the boat is on the water and water is, among other things, the symbol for emotions. This illustration reinforces the idea that there will have to be an inner transformation... Furthermore, water, sea and ocean refer to the mother, the inner mother, your birth mother, the Celestial Mother, the Mother of Mothers... Anyway, there is no difference. The outer Self is like the inner Self. Water reflects like a mirror. However, be careful not to agitate the lower depths too much, because who knows what will come to the surface or what you are going to see, feel and hear!

This illustration leads me to talk about the "Law of Vibration". The "Law of Vibration" refers, among others, to our vibratory rate and to the one that emanates when we create, talk and so on. Through communication and creativity, we send out to the entire Universe, a vibratory rate X according to what we have communicated and created. Once again, this is a good reason not to communicate or create with low energy vibrations. Otherwise, what we receive will also be at a low vibration. In contrast, when you are a medium (we *All* are), and you want to convey messages from deceased loved ones who are necessarily in a low vibration, you must also be in a low vibratory level just like them. In other words, if, for example, you want to hear or see Angels, you must have a higher vibratory rate or raise your vibratory rate. Since my lifestyle allows me to raise my vibration, I can work with both groups and I only have to lower my vibratory rate to be able to receive messages from deceased loved ones. However, please note that a psychic who eats meat, drinks alcohol and smokes, for example, will be able to receive messages from deceased loved ones too, in particular those who had alcohol and smoking problems, but may not necessarily receive messages from Light beings, Angels or Archangels. Be careful, you might meet a deceased alcohol or drug addict that might try to take your energy, who knows? Archangels and Angels can lower their frequency, but only down to a certain point. If you want to hear or see them, you must meet them half way.

We *All* vibrate at various frequencies according to how we live. Going back to the symbolism of the boat, in the autumn of 2009, I went on a cruise to take a course: "Spirit Connexion Caribbean Cruise" with Lisa Williams and John Holland, two internationally renowned mediums. I was really in my element. I am a fairy or a nature Angel, so I Love water. When I was younger, I spent *All* my summers at Lac St-François (St-Francis Lac). I was in training. I Love to study, learn and expand my numerous talents. Besides, I was with hundreds of people who shared my interest in Mediumship. Lisa Williams and John Holland, in addition to being psychics, are also authors. *All* the elements were gathered to Light my fire within. My inner flame, my passion was burning with *All* its fires. I would say that about mid-week I woke up in the middle of the night and my solar plexus area was illuminated. I saw a bright white Light coming from that area and, when I put my hands on it, I could see an orange-reddish coloured aura around my hands. It was fun to put my hands in front of the Light and to take them off. I was overwhelmed by the magic of the moment.

Later on, I had the opportunity to meet "Maitreyi Amma" (a Divinity with energy similar to that of the Holy Mother Mary or Kwan Yin), June 12 and 13, 2010 in Montreal. On Sunday afternoon, we could meet her and ask questions. I asked her what she thought about my experience of illumination. According to her, I was experiencing, at that moment, illumination in the solar plexus area because that is the region where our emotions are and this was an illustration of purification inside of me. I still have a lot of purification to do and consequently I still need a flashlight in the dark. Ha! Ha! I do not "glow in the dark" yet. It is a shame because I could reduce my electricity bill.

In Tarot, the Empress, represents the "Law of Vibration". She is the archetype of the mother, the one who protects, creates and advises. She is the feminine equivalent of the Emperor. The Empress and the Emperor are one of the three couples that exist in Tarot. She inspires, imagines, dreams and he materializes. He is an entrepreneur, a man of action. She communicates in writing or verbally. The Empress is the Arcanum number 3 and corresponds to the third house in astrology. The third house in astrology is the house of communication, *know*ledge and travel... My first name is Chantal. It starts with a C and the letter C corresponds to 3 in numerology, thus communication, *know*ledge and travel. That explains my interest in everything involving written or verbal communication and my passion for studying and traveling. This reinforces the fact that *All* the elements were gathered together during the cruise in the Caribbean, communication (with the Spirits), *know*ledge (the course), and travel. I have a friend who often teases me by saying that if studying had been a job option; I would certainly have opted for this kind of job. I Love to study. Currently, however, I do not study in the same way. Now, I do not necessarily end up in the same subject that I start studying or reading. I simply listen to my intuition and follow it. I am often guided to read about information I need without knowing at the time that I will use it later on. This could be information for me or for another person, a client, a friend, or even to write this book, for example. I receive information I will need in the future. Here, we are talking more about the "Law of Attraction", or would it be the "Law of Vibration"? Attraction or Vibration? Are we Attracting what we vibrate or are we Vibrating what we attract? That is the REAL question! "Two pieces of robot*" for whoever finds the answer!

*Refers to a television show (Satellipopettes) where the participants received pieces of robots when they answered the questions they were asked correctly... the goal was to complete the entire robot by the end of the show.

Personal applications

In this chapter, the subject is also related to a *social action resonance*, because we are referring to the Empress. This is a person who does not use her full power and is certainly not acting according to her own free will. She doesn't know how to express herSelf. There are a lot of problems with communication and sensitivity to be found here. We can also relate her to the kind of person who has a lot of trouble making decisions, who lacks spirit and lives in in-*action*. She is very tough and embodies addiction, submission and timidity in every aspect of her person. She often thinks she is wrong because of her great sense of inferiority. When she believes she is superior, she may abuse her own power or be very authoritarian... if and of course only if, there are emotional blockages. Otherwise, someone who vibrates in a vortex of positive energy grows with an enormous power, great desire and knowledge of how to express herSelf. She does not have any communication problems, and she also knows how to express her sensitivity, since she has great power of emotional expression. The strength to fight flows in her veins; she possesses great personal power and a lot of enthusiasm. She always achieves what she wants with effort, initiative and a lot of respect for her responsibilities. She has great power. She exercises her own free will. She acts. She has influence. She demands. She is. She is in her own place... that is *All*!

To determine if there is an emotional blockage in your personal life, I suggest you take the time to answer the following questions honestly:

✓ **Are you someone who does not use All your personal** *power*?

If not, why not?

When, in your life, are you weak?

How do you know you are not using *All* your *power*?

You have probably experienced a sense of *power* in your life.

If that is the case, I would ask you to re-visit that moment and to experience that great sense of *power*... re-live that experience here and now... yes, very well... re-live it... Hear what there is to hear... music... people talking... surrounding noises... Feel what there is to feel... an emotion... a sensation... heat... cold... inside your body... and out... See what there is to see... a colour... people... around you... and inside. Now, combine *All* the elements that constitute this wonderful experience and form them into a shape... a form... a symbol... a colour... an emotion... a smell... a flavour... a name... whatever... They are *All* symbols... The goal here is for you to have access to that symbol any time and to *All* the benefits of this experience of great *power*, whenever you want. Now, take this symbol... place it where you can access it in the future, when you need it... that's it, very well... Now, remember an experience in which you felt weak. As soon as you start to feel... see... hear... this experience... call on your symbol of strength and great *power*... Feel *All* the benefits of great *power* in *All* the cells of your being... When you feel that you now have total *control*... I would again ask you to remember another experience when you felt weak... As soon as you start to feel... see... hear... this experience... call on your symbol of strength and great *power*... Feel *All* the benefits of great *power* in *All* the cells of your being... and when you feel that you have total *power*... I would again ask you to remember another experience when you were weak... As soon as you start to feel ... see ... hear this experience call on your symbol of *strength* and great *power*... Feel *All* the benefits of great *power* in *All* the cells of your being and when you feel that you have complete *power*... Stay in that state for as long as you wish and when you truly experiences a feeling of great power, then you have succeeded. You can practice this exercise whenever you will feel weak in the future... Now you are embodied with a great *power*!

✓ **Do you act according to your *own free will*?**

If not, why not?

Do you think there are positive consequences if you do? What are they?

If you acted according to your *own free will*, what would happen?

What would your friends think?

Are there negative consequences for you?

In your opinion, is it dis-honest not to act according to our *own free will*?

If so, then what exactly do you think about it?

What are the consequences according to you?

Do you think you are being dis-*respectful* to yourSelf when you do not act according to your *own free will*?

Suppose that we are on Earth to learn, experiment and to release some karmas and we don't act according to our *own free will* in this present life, which is probably why we are here now. If we do not resolve that problem in this life, we will have to experience it again in another life. What do you think? Do you really want to go through *All* this again?

✓ **Do you have a lot of difficulty *expressing* yourSelf?**

Do you have *communication* problems?

Do you know the Source of your *communication* problems?

Do you remember the first time you started to have difficulties *communicating*?

When do you find it hardest to *express* yourSelf?

There is a saying that night advises. I suggest you simply ask to be guided by your dreams.

Here is an example of what you could write:

"Tonight, I am going to consult my dreams to find out how to *express* mySelf in a better way. Thank you."

Write an intentional note like this one and put it next to you on your beside table, for example. You can keep it there as long as you wish. When you wake up in the morning, you will have the information needed to improve your *communication* skills. However, if life considers that you have more important things to settle at present, it will probably not answer your request. That is why I suggest you leave the paper there for a while. It is better to get more information then not enough. If you do not analyze your dreams, don't worry because you have issued an intentional note to the Universe and you will receive a response no matter what. The only thing you have to do is send a special request and you will receive an answer to your prayers! Just say thank you to the Universe! And be receptive...

✓ **Do you have problems with *sensitivity*?**

Are you too *sensitive* or not *sensitive* enough?

Often, we have to experience extremes to become more balanced.

Do you consider yourSelf more Yin or more Yang?

Do you think this has an effect on your ability to be *sensitive*?

If you are in-*sensitive*, what are you protecting yourSelf from?

Have you ever experienced a situation that caused you harm and could be responsible for your need to protect yourSelf and has made you in-*sensitive* and afraid of being hurt again?

Are you afraid you might be considered weak if you are *sensitive*?

If you are hyper-*sensitive*, do you feel as if you were transgressed?

In your life, when do you think you feel transgressed?

What do you do to protect yourSelf against that transgression?

How do you reduce your *sensitivity*?

The "seat of our emotions" is the solar plexus which is strongly connected to creation and Power. The chakra in this region is a yellowish hue in colour. When there is a blockage in this area, the chakra will be too small or too big, perhaps mottled or turning counter clockwise. Take the time to visualize... hear... feel... your solar plexus chakra located in the middle of your body above the sternum... Is it a beautiful shade of yellow or are there some black or grey spots in it? Is it too big or too small compared to the other chakras? The chakras must *All* be the same size, the size you are guided to... Ask it to be at the normal frequency. Is it turning the wrong way? The chakras should normally turn clockwise. Ask your chakra to be purified... See it as a bright beautiful shade of yellow... Imagine its frequency being restored, turning normally, clockwise... Repeat this exercise every day for as long as you need to. Enjoy the experience and collect *All* the information concerning your *sensibility*.

✓ **Do you have a hard time making *decisions*?**

If so, when have you had trouble making *decisions*?

Why do you think you have such a hard time *deciding*?

Have you ever experienced a situation where you did not have any trouble *deciding*?

I would ask you to re-live this experience in which making a *decision* was easy... Everything was easy for you at that moment... Re-live that experience intensely: see it... hear it... feel it... Now, write down everything you are re-living... Everything you see... hear... feel. Are you associated (are you in your body)? Do you see yourSelf from within? Alternately, are you disassociated (do you see yourSelf from outside)? Are you outside your own body? What colours do you see? Are they bright or dark? Is it night or day? What do you see around you? Write it *All* down... Write down whatever you are feeling... your emotions... feelings... heat... cold... write it *All* down... Write whatever you hear... music... noises... voices... thoughts... inner voices... guides... write it *All* down. Then, re-live an experience in which you were unable to decide... Re-live that experience... See it... hear it... feel it... Now, write it *All* down. Everything you see. Are you associated (Are you in your own body)? Do you see yourSelf from within? Alternately, are you disassociated (do you see yourSelf from outside)? Are you outside your own body? What colours do you see? Are they bright or dark? Is it night or day? What do you see around you? Write it *All* down... Write down whatever you are feeling: your emotions... feelings... heat... cold... write it *All* down...Write down whatever you hear... music... noises... voices... thoughts... inner voices... guides... write it *All* down...

Finally, draw a table like this one and compare the differences.

EXPERIENCE	HARD TO MAKE A DECISION	*EASY TO MAKE A DECISION*
WHAT I SEE	I am disassociated (I see myself from outside my body) Dark colours, Night	I am associated (I'm in my own body, I see through my own eyes) Luminous colours, Day
WHAT I FEEL	Stress Nervous Unbalanced Ill Scared	Well being Pride Joy Power Happiness Harmony
WHAT I HEAR	Negative thoughts, Negative and pessimistic lyrics	Positive thoughts, Positive and optimistic lyrics, Birds singing, Music, Encouragement from others

What do you notice?

Are there differences between your experiences?

Now, imagine a decision you will have to make in the future. Write down what you see, feel and hear at that moment. Then compare your notes with the ones in the table. This table permits you to re-focus. If you are experiencing difficulty making a decision, re-arrange your environment with the standards in the table under the column "*Easy to make a decision*". Re-*connect* yourSelf mentally to your experience of finding it *easy to make a decision*. If, for example, you are dis-*associated* when you experience difficulty making a *decision*, then associate yourSelf entirely. Take the time to really feel your body. Ground yourSelf to Mother-Earth by visualizing roots coming out of your feet and entering the ground. Feel the energy flowing from the Earth into your body through the roots... This way, you will inhabit your own body. Automatically, you will re-live *All* the characteristics of making a decision easily one after the other. I suggest that in the future you should pay attention to *All* your experiences of decision making and evaluate them. Re-focusing will come naturally with time and patience; without even thinking about it!

P.S.: There is an extraordinary stone used for focusing. The Staurolite or fairy cross, its symbolism is " The stone of crossroads (of choices)", (English translation of the French statement: « La pierre du Carrefour des choix»), p.313 *Dictionnaire de Lithothérapie.* "These little stones formed following the crucifixion of Christ. Fairies' tears would have formed the stones when their tears dropped onto crystals because of the death of Jesus Christ on the cross. That is why the stones are in the shape of crosses." (English translation of French statement: «On raconte que ces petites macles auraient été formées suite à la crucifixion du Christ. Les fées auraient formé ces macles par leurs larmes déversées sur des cristaux, à cause de la mort du Seigneur sur la croix. Voilà pourquoi, les macles sont en forme de croix.»). I have one and it is a pendant which I wear on a necklace. They are easy to purify, simply bury them in earth; they Love it.

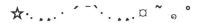

Chapter 4

REALIZATION

❋

The High Priestess or Female Pope devotes herSelf to spirituality, and the inner world. The Emperor is the embodiment of action. The Empress is the symbol of creativity and communication. The Emperor indicates that we must accept responsibility for what we have created in the past. The Empress, under the vibrations of the number 3, represents concepts or ideas. The Emperor, under the ascendancy of number 4, represents stability, but no longer the concept or the idea. What was thought, imagined or dreamed has now materialized. What is upstairs is also downstairs... Having faith that we can do it *All*, believing that we are a creation, and a channel to communicate LOVE, then we must take action.

We are dealing here with the archetype of the father; the father who is a protector. He protects what belongs to him... The question he must ask himself is: "What really belongs to me?" The answer is NOTHING but, he protects anyway. He brings a lot of stability and he is the type who is an entrepreneur, a leader. In contrast, the Empress is a woman of heart, whereas the Emperor is a man of mind. He is a purveyor of intellectual and rational thought. However, he has been chosen by the people!

In this chapter, we will look at the "Law of Realization", which is the masculine aspect in every human being. The feminine vision has Yin energy, which is a softer energy, but lazier. She is the dreamer. The male vision has Yang energy. This is the part of your being that puts what has been imagined by the feminine part into action. It is the part that gives birth. After having meditated, prayed, dreamed, or imagined, we have to make real what is still in the in-*visible* world. This principle is the balance. We have received, now we must give back in return. Otherwise, watch out for the congestion...

As I have already mentioned, I receive a lot of information through my dreams at night. One night, because I placed the card of the Emperor on my bedside table, I received some advice through my dreams concerning my advertising in the newspaper "Le Soleil de Valleyfield". In my dream, I saw how I could advertise mySelf in a completely different way, but... I had to wait to receive a second sign which would be a day sign this time. A few days later, the newspaper's publicist called me to inform me of her new concept for advertising. It was exactly what I had seen in my dream. Fabulous isn't it?

Another night, I dreamed I received a white wand full of spikes with *All* the colours of the rainbow. This wand was given to me by none other than Jesus, my Guide. It was smaller and softer in his hands and looked like a snake. However, once in my hands, it became longer and harder just like wood. With this wand, I felt I was going to succeed at whatever I wanted to do, no matter what. Is it a magic wand? This story reminds me of the famous wooden stick that Moses had... furthermore, the snake is curled around a wooden stick on the emblem of medicine! Jesus and Moses are examples of people who heard God's messages clearly and transmitted what they received. In my prayers, I often ask Jesus and Moses to help me hear and understand the messages that God addresses to me clearly and to have a better relationship with Him. Is this a sign or an answer to my prayers? Are they passing me the stick? The talking stick... The healing stick perhaps... Uh!

-._.- *-._.-* *-._.-* *-._.-* *-._.-* *-._.-*

In numerology the number 3 relates to balance: the balance between intelligence, emotion and will. Therefore, the number 4 relates to stability and realization. However, before we reach stability and realization... we must be in harmony. Or rather, we have to be well balanced and harmonized to be stable and well realized. This brings to mind the idea of the chakras which are small disks or wheels of energy, vibrating at a frequency according to the chakra in question and its opening. The chakras are centers of energy located at the level of the spine (five principals), between the eyes (third eye chakra) and on the top of the head (crown chakra). These are the seven major chakras. Some authors claim that there could be up to twenty-eight chakras and even more. Here we are also talking about the chakras found in our body's energy field on the outside of the physical body, in our aura. We have chakras beneath our feet, around our being and above our head. When they are in harmony, I believe the twenty-eight chakras allow us to be well grounded to Mother-Earth and also *connected* to our Father-Sun, just like a tree... a link between the Sky and the Earth... like a rainbow. The rainbow is visible when conditions are favourable. When our chakras are well harmonized, we become like a rainbow... a Union between this world and the rest of the Universe.

The Emperor assumes responsibility for what he has created or produced. As a result, we are able to see the consequences of our thoughts, words, deeds, wishes, desires... The mother who over-protects her child, for example, bites her fingers when what she was afraid of finally happens. She spent a lot of energy not wanting something to happen to her child. Remember that energy sent out into the Universe always returns to its Source, whether it is good or bad. For example, when a mother says to her child "put your coat on, or you will catch a cold...", and in the end the child catches a cold, what was she expecting? She asked for it! Don't be surprised if what you are most afraid of happens. You waste a lot of energy on fear... Afraid to be afraid! I know a girl who is very frightened of sharks. She was in the Ocean in Mexico. She saw sharks everywhere, even where there were no sharks. She almost drowned because of her fear. She imagined she saw a shark, but the fish was, in fact, the size of a sardine. I also know a man who, for years, kept repeating to his girlfriend that she was going to leave him to live with a doctor. He was right; she left him, but... to heal herSelf and to become a healing channel, so yes, she is now living with a doctor!

That is a very good way to illustrate the fact that we must accept responsibility for what we have created in our life. We are lucky because there are several ways to fix what we have created, if what we have created is wrong and if we recognize it is wrong. Personally, I think that the simplest way is to surround the event, situation, person, group of people or yourSelf with a beautiful, bright, white Light. The white Light neutralizes the situation. The Light is LOVE, *know*ledge and white includes *All* the colours of the rainbow. Therefore, I wish you an abundance of beautiful and bright Light!

Personal Applications

In this chapter, the subject is also related to social influence resonance, because we are referring to the Emperor. Here we are referring to the type of person who is unable to use *All* the power in her heart. She only acts with her mind. Her energy is centered in her mind. This is a person lacking greatly in humanity, who has many problems with stability and method. We are also talking about a person who is very closed, selfish and lacks courage. She embodies dishonesty. She is very distant and sometimes melancholic. She often feels excluded and abandoned. She does not appreciate what she has and is ungrateful... if and of course only if, there are emotional blockages. Otherwise, someone who vibrates in a vortex of positive energy will hear the voice of her heart as well as her own feelings. Love of liberty and interest in others are some of her characteristics. She is a humanitarian, in harmony and brave in *All* her sensitivity. This type of person works in a positive way and is naturally open, honest and has a lot of sympathy. She is a Source of pure LOVE, that is to say, Unconditional LOVE. She is LOVE. She honours. She forgives. She shares *All* with you from her heart and not just her mind. Bring it *All* to the heart and you will heal! Remember to learn to forgive! Forgiveness is one of the keys to being open!

To determine if there is an emotional blockage in your personal life, I suggest you take the time to answer the following questions honestly:

✓ **Do you follow the path of your *heart*?**

Or do you follow your head instead?

If so, when do you follow your mind's path?

Why do you follow your mind instead of your *heart*?

If you act with your mind rather than your *heart*, are you doing it with LOVE?

Do you feel that your *heart* is blocked or simply closed?

If so, then I suggest you buy a stone or crystal. *All* green or pink stones and crystals are related to the *heart* chakra and can be wonderfully healing. You could follow your *heart* and go and buy one, or, you could do some research beforehand. Here are some suggestions:

Green Aventurine	Green Sapphire	Pink Topaz
Emerald	Green Tourmaline	Rhodochrosite
Green Fluorite	Pink Tourmaline	Pink Quartz
Malachite	Watermelon Tourmaline	And much more!

✓ **Do you live an absence of *humanity*?**

If so, when do you feel you lack *humanity*?

Have you ever shown interest in others?

Interest and compassion for others are essential characteristics to a person's *humanity*.

In your opinion, what is the first step you could take to bring more *humanity* into your life today?

✓ **Do you tend to feel un-*stable*?**

If so, when do you experience in-*stability*?

When you experience in-*stability*, are you in your head or elsewhere in your body?

Bring that feeling of in-*stability* to the level of your heart. Wrap this feeling with the colour of a pink hue... Wrap it with tenderness, gentleness, compassion and service to others... What do you feel now? You could also enhance the situation with the scent of roses. Pretend you can smell some beautiful, pink roses... Pink roses are flowers associated with the heart chakra. In the future, every time you recall a feeling of in-*stability*, bring that feeling to the level of your heart and wrap it in the colour pink and the scent of pink roses. The feeling will fade and eventually disappear. Repeat the exercise until you feel more *stable* in a lasting way!

N.B.: For best results, I suggest you:

1. Buy yourself a real rose for the exercise; you will enjoy its colour and scent; (see its beauty)

2. Alternatively, buy an essential oil of roses. You can put on a few drops, use it in a diffuser, or simply smell it, that way you will enjoy it longer than a real rose and whenever you wish!

✓ **Do you think you are a *methodical* person?**

If so, how?

In your opinion, what is the definition of *methodical*? In other words, define a *methodical* person?

Have you ever had an experience in your life when you were *methodical*?

Many things you have learned in life are based on *method*. When you learned to walk, you did it gradually, one step at a time. Step by step. *Methodically*. The same thing happened for *All* the learning that you have experienced during your life, therefore, somewhere inside you is a *methodical* person. To develop your *methodical* side, I suggest you do an activity that will improve this facet in you. Anything that requires *method* is recommended here, it could be... painting, building something, learning a language, writing, gathering something... Then, develop it according to your own *method*!

✓ **Are you a closed minded person?**

If you are, re-call an experience when you felt confident enough to have the power to express your real Self without fear? At that moment, you were able to be just the person you wanted to be... at that moment you could really express yourSelf... and you knew nobody could hurt you in any way. Trust and faith were kings at that moment.

Notice the differences that you live now compared to that moment. What do you find?

What could have created this closed mindedness?

Can you find wellness in your life today?

If not, re-*connect* to the heart of your inner child. Relive the *openness* of a child... your own inner child... without barriers. Ask and your wish will be fulfilled! It is the only child you really own!

✓ **Do you tend to tell lies?**

If so, why do you do it?

What is preventing you from telling the *truth*?

Are you afraid of the *truth*?

You know, you cannot escape the *truth*. It will emerge, make no mistake! No matter what game you play, it will re-surface and it might look you right in the face.

It is written in the book *A Course In Miracles*: « The *Truth* will correct *All* the mistakes in your mind... » According to the teachings of Jesus Christ, only the *truth* exists and everything else is illusion. Illusions will eventually be destroyed and the *truth* will be revealed. Anyway, by this game, you will attract the same kind of energy to yourSelf. One day you will need to hear the *truth* from someone you really care about and what you will hear are the lies you have been creating. It is never too late to start cultivating the seeds of *truth*! What are you waiting for?

✓ **Do you tend to suffer from melancholy?**

Does melancholy tend to surface very often in your life?

If so, then tell me what makes you *happy*?

When will you be able to do whatever brings you *joy* whenever you want?

Buddha, Cordelia, Isis and John of God are examples of Deities who can guide us toward *joy*. Simply invoke them. They are here to help us. Pray and they will hear you. Ask and they will respond. On the other hand, you must truly want their help. Do not just pronounce words without feelings. See what you are asking for and feel the *joy* already inside you... listen to what you are hearing when you are *happy*... Send Love to these Deities through your heart to thank them... see the energy moving from you towards them... and feel what happens in the days to come as you... return to the Source!

✓ **Do you feel abandoned?**

Have you often felt abandoned in your life?

According to Caroline Myss, in her book *Sacred Contracts*, we *All* have the archetype of the victim in us. We have *All* been victims at some time... And many of us have been victims of abandonment. This event is the cause of several other events created precisely because of this first event. Remember, we attract what we are...

I suggest that you return to the precise moment when you lived your first experience of being abandoned; in this life or in another. Ask to re-live, here and now, your first experience of being abandoned... Re-live the experience now... see the experience of being abandoned... feel it... hear it ... see what there is to see... feel what there is to feel... hear what there is to hear... If you receive images, symbols or anything else from your imagination don't stop them, because imagination is a form of clairvoyance... Now, correct the scene... re-arrange your environment... do whatever you want to do so you will have a better experience. You now know that imagination is reality. A genius imagines first before his creations come to life, so what you imagine most also eventually manifests itSelf. You are the creator of your own experiences, so create your new experience the way you want it to be... Add some elements... subtract some elements... play with your emotions and add whatever you want so that you feel the way you would like to feel. Improve your experience... now you are feeling exactly the way you imagined you would feel. From now on, you will no longer feel abandoned because you have created a whole new destiny where abandonment does not exist!

✓ Do you have trouble forgiving others?

I suggest you look at the twelve Steps of Forgiveness described by Paul Ferrini in his book *The 12 Steps of FORGIVENESS - A Practical Manual for Moving from Fear to Love*... a tiny book of only a hundred pages, but very rich in *know*ledge. Here are the suggested twelve steps to forgiveness:

1. "Recognize the fear;
2. Understand it's Love that you want;
3. Withdraw the projection;
4. Take responsibility;
5. Release self-judgment and guilt;
6. Accept yourself and others as you are;
7. Be willing to learn and share;
8. Be your own authority;
9. Accept the lesson;
10. See that everything is okay as it is;
11. Look in the mirror;
12. Open your heart."

Take the time needed to analyze these steps and to use them in a way that will allow you to forgive, so you can move from fear to Love!

In the book *A Course in Miracles,* it is taught that there are only two types of emotions: fear and Love. So when you are afraid, re-focus on Love. Love makes everything possible! Love heals everything! Love is everything!

Chapter 5

INSPIRATION

The High Priestess, Empress, Emperor and Pope are *All* arcana figures in tarot and reflect personality characteristics. These are archetypes that affect, directly or in-directly, the physical or spiritual being. Their resonance makes us understand our social involvement in this world. Now that we have looked at spirituality, communication and realization, we are ready for the teaching stage. Does that make us a student or a teacher? Personally, I think that they both happen in the same way. However, are we looking for a Master or are we the Master?

The Pope, the fifth Arcanum in tarot, is associated with the "Law of Inspiration". We can feel his inspiration through his passion and desire for Union with the Divine; a Source of fire; fire of the Soul; the Divine and Eternal mystic flame; the wonder of the Soul... which can be seen and felt in the aura or energy through whomever it transpires. Often at night, in our dreams we can be shown the excitement of our Soul through eroticism, for example. Eroticism, physical enjoyment, physical movement that your Soul chooses to express satisfaction and joy! Live the life that YOU have chosen to live!

The Pope is the Arcanum figure that corresponds to the fifth astrological house where we find creativity, gifts, sexuality and children. Because we have already discussed sexuality, we will now talk about creativity. This Arcanum reminds us of our creative power. Creativity expresses both the wonders and chaos engendered by our imagination. Thus, our inner transformation is unmasked by our creativity. No matter what we express and how we express it, we are always talking about ourselves.

The "Law of Inspiration" reminds me of a thought that I like. The general idea is that a successful person is someone who is a Source of inspiration for others. Personally, I think that from the moment we act with passion, we are a Source of inspiration because what we do is done with Love. Passion is Love.

This Arcanum resonates greatly with me for several reasons. The first reason is that I identify a lot with the archetype of the student. That is why, among other things, it took me so long to write this book. Fear of not being ready, fear of not knowing enough and fear of not being up to the standard. Wilrose, my ex-father in law, used to say that studying for me was comparable to gasoline in a vehicle; it was vital for me. I can only confirm this hypothesis: studying and learning are my essence. I stopped studying for a few months and I will never do that again. However, I do feel I have a responsibility to transmit my *know*ledge and experiences to others, which gives me a lot of joy. I Love sharing what I learn. What I am learning now is very different. I am developing my spiritual gifts and abilities and I have realized that people around me are also developing their gifts. Moreover, their gifts are strangely similar to mine. A coincidence, probably! What kind of Law is involved here? The law of Attraction? Vibration? Inspiration? All three? Perhaps it is the Law of transpiration? Ha! Ha!

Joking aside! The Pope is an archetype that resonates a lot with me because, in another life, I was a Pope; a dictator Pope if you know what I mean. The kind that imposes his ideas and beliefs, which is why, in this life, I am guided to help others on their spiritual path. I appear in their life when they need to re-

connect to their Souls, recognize their life mission and develop their gifts. I apply the different Laws of the Spirit daily. These are not religious, but rather spiritual Laws. I study various teachings of Christ from several Sources, but the One I prefer is: *A Course In Miracles*.

In numerology, the number 5 is attributed to inspiration and it is also the number attributed to man. Inspiration is the reflection of Divine perfection at the very center of man which is the center of the Universe and its Source! Where everything is... And the Pope knows that what is found above is also found below. And he knows that what is outside is also inside. Re-flection... He knows that deep down, it is *All* the same and we are *All* United. The more we study the more we realize that everything is inter-*connected*. As in the sea depths, the deeper we go the more likely we are to discover buried treasures. He is not afraid to go deeper and deeper. He knows because he has a lot of *know*ledge; *know*ledge that he has carried with him for a very long time. Where are his gifts, creativity, sexuality and his children, sm-*All* or t-*All*. His Source of fire; His mystic flame; His wonders; His miracles; His disasters; His teachings; His healing; His evolution; His education. And, at some point, in due course, he will decide to teach whoever asks him.

The greatest teacher I have had is Jesus Christ, although *All* my teachers have been excellent and I would like to thank them *All*. Jesus Christ is my Guide and I had difficulty admitting it for a long period of time. I thought my imagination was playing tricks on me. I thought "Why me? Why would Jesus be MY Guide?" You can imagine the scene. Then I understood and decided to move forward with him at my side as I was supposed to. He can be your Guide too, you only have to ask. We *All* have Christ inside us. We must recognize this first and then we will recognize God. In order to reach God, we must go through Christ. To find the father, we must first see the son. We are the sons and daughters of God. Christ illustrates our origins, our essence, our Divine Self and our Luminous Self. He shows us that we are made in the image of God; the one that is perfect. As long as you are not afraid of heights... afraid of happiness... afraid of Love... afraid of inner balance... As it is taught in *A Course In Miracles* there are only two emotions: Love and fear and fear is the opposite of Love. I suggest that you think twice before being afraid the next time you are frightened. Love heals *All*!

Personal Applications

In this chapter, there is also a resonance influence. Resonance at the place that the person holds in society, the work she must do on a material and spiritual level, because we are relating to the Arcanum figure of The Pope. Several types of archetypes may be involved: the student, the teacher, the master and the guide as well as the guru, the charlatan and the founder of a sect. This is a person who may use the voice of the un-*conscious*, the voice of the Ego. This person acts out of fear. She only uses her energy to defend herself. She blocks a lot. She is the type of person who is lacking self abandonment and has many problems with freedom and discipline. She has a lot of obsessions, lacks spontaneity and lives in fear of death. She embodies rigidity and falsehood. She is very stubborn and very controlling. She often feels denied, victimized and helpless. She loves to be the centre of attention. She is united, according to her, to the only part of herself, her Ego... if and of course only if, there are emotional blockages. Otherwise, a person who is under the influence of positive energy speaks words of truth and uses her own divinity. She will act with Love. She will not use *All* her energy to defend herSelf. Devoted, she expresses herSelf with a touch of creativity and knows how to communicate well. She is *connected* to her childhood heart, allowing her to play and have a lot of fun with great spontaneity. Self abandonment and Self *know*ledge are Kings and Masters here. She is like a butterfly with *All* its lightness and expressiveness. She knows how to surrender. She manifests herSelf. She is open minded. She shows herSelf. She is true. She lets go and that is how she can hear God's voice bringing words of Truth, Love, Joy, Harmony and Peace... "And may Peace be with her, since she is finally spreading her wings!"

To determine if there is an emotional blockage in your personal life, I suggest you take the time to answer the following questions honestly:

✓ **Are you fearful?**

Are you often frightened?

What do you fear?

According to the teachings of *A Course In Miracles* there are only two types of emotion, *Love* and fear. When we are afraid, we do not feel the emotion *Love*. Moreover, according to the teachings of this book, when we experience negative energy, we are in a world of illusion. Anything that is contrary to *Love* is illusion; fears are illusions. Because you create your own reality, I would ask you to think for a moment about how you could change your reality...

Here is an example: I was afraid of the dark, especially when I was alone or in an unfamiliar place. To solve this problem, I called upon the Archangel Michael. The Archangel Michael protects against anything that is negative. He defends. He has a sword with which he cuts down any Source affecting the positive development of a person. As soon as he appears, you see the room Lighting up. Thus, if you call upon him during the night, he will hunt the shadows and protect against the negative.

Now, think about how you could replace fear with *Love* in your life today? Trust yourSelf, you are an intelligent person and will find a way...

✓ **Do you constantly need to defend yourSelf?**

Do you often feel attacked?

Against whom are you fighting?

Do you defend your rights and freedom?

What do you protect at *All* costs?

Do you protect or over-protect?

Are you the one attacking?

Yes? Do not be surprised then if you are attacked. This is simply *'your just deserts'*. Remember, whatever energy is sent out into the Universe always returns to its Source! ...returning to the Source!

✓ **Are you someone who obstructs a lot?**

If so, where in your life do you obstruct? Why?

What are the benefits?

What are the dis-advantages?

If you decide to stop obstructing, what would be the side effects?

Could this be harmful to your environment?

What would the people around you think?

So, is it still useful to obstruct?

Imagine that this blockage is a locked door. You hold the key to unlock that door which has been closed for a long time. Unlock the door with the key you hold. Access to that beautiful key is not given to *All*... but you own it. Opening the door makes you feel liberated and lighter. When you open the door, you breathe fresh air. You feel released... as if you had wings on your feet now... open at your own rhythm each closed doors that is blocking your life... You will finally enjoy great freedom!

✓ **Are you someone who does not surrender easily?**

Do you have trouble *letting go*?

Is it possible you want to control too much?

Are you so wise that you are unable to experience pleasure?

Is it a lack of confidence or faith?

I suggest that you try an exercise to help you *abandon yourSelf*. Either standing or sitting, whichever is more comfortable for you, put on some music and move your body to the beat without using premeditated gestures or movements. Go ahead without thinking. "BODYFLOW" is like a dream dance with your eyes closed. This type of exercise allows you to *let go*; controlling nothing at *All* and experiencing pleasure. Finally, try to catch the stars with your hands. Do this for a few minutes. Touch the stars... you are made of star dust! So, you are a star! *Abandon yourSelf* to the thousands of stars of life!

✓ **Do you lack *discipline* in your life?**

If so, when do you lack *discipline*?

What could you do to correct this lack of *discipline*?

Is it lack of *discipline* or motivation?

If it is lack of motivation, then what motivates you?

How can you integrate a Source of motivation into your activities and be more *disciplined*?

Here is an example: personally, I lacked *discipline* while doing my morning workouts. I love music and singing, so I combined *All* three: I do my workouts while listening to music and singing. This way I give mySelf a huge kick in the behind, because each of these activities is a great Source of energy for me. Just imagine *All* three together! It was so exhilarating that at first I was doing my workout every morning and now I have to restrict it to every other day, because the excess energy created insomnia! Furthermore, the exercises I do are to *awaken* the Kundalini and the chakras. In other words, these exercises allow for a better flow of energy... *discipline* too because it allows for better *knowl*edge of the subject and freedom to listen, feel and see more deeply and be among the best!

✓ **Are you afraid of death?**

Do you believe in *life after death*?

If not, why?

Let me tell you some true stories.

During my Caribbean cruise with Lisa Williams and John Holland, we could clearly see the Spirits with them on the stage. They used a blue light similar to a "black light" on a white background. This way we could see (with our own eyes) the Spirits who wanted to communicate with their loved ones through Lisa and John. Even sceptics saw the Spirits. During this course, I had the opportunity to meet a lady who lives in Gaspésie. At first she was sceptical, but she saw them too. Most of us do not tend to believe everything that touches the in-*visible* world, since we do not see it. In spirituality, we must believe first and after we will be able to see. This is a golden rule! As in everyday life, we bring our dreams to life because we believe in them. Dreams are also a part of the in-*visible* world at first. This world becomes *visible* when we believe in it.

Fifteen years ago, Michel, my life partner, had a near death experience; he suffered a cardiac arrest during surgery when he was diagnosed with cancer. He was floating above the operating table. He could hear what the doctors and the rest of the medical team were saying. His Spirit was separated from his physical body and it fluttered into the room. This is an example of what happens when we die. There are transformations of the physical envelope so we can live different experiences, but our Soul, our Spirit, never dies.

Finally, I personally see Spirits and Light beings. I feel them and sometimes I hear them. When they want to reveal themselves, I can see their faces in "flashes' in my imagination and through my third eye. On the other hand, very often, I see energy moving or as if I see moving shapes, translucent just like water. I feel a draft, a drop in temperature or something that touches me. Very often, I see sparkles, violet or blue Light beings, everywhere I go. Some authors call this phenomenon "orb" and I think it is very close to what I see. Orbs could be clues that a Light being is nearby. They do not reveal themselves entirely. If they did, just imagine your reaction! They start by showing a small part of their identity. I find it realistic, because over the years, the small circles of Light I see have grown a lot. Furthermore, I pray every day and I frequently ask for their help; help with writing, for example. They are revealed to me more and more and I must say that I am no longer afraid...

N.B: Cordierite or iolite is a stone that helps repel, emotionally and mentally, the anguish caused by fear of death...

Chapter 6

THE INNER COUPLE
♀ ♂

Energy aspires to move, more and more, towards an energy that is centered on Love. When people talk about the changes for 2012, they are talking about an energy metamorphosis. For a long time energy was predominantly male; a yang energy. But for a period of time now, energy has tended more and more towards being a female energy; yin energy.

When I was younger, I heard older people say that women would lead the world one day. Now, I understand that they were not necessarily talking about the physical being but rather Universal energy. We *All* know that in most homes it is the woman who decides, which should not be the case in my opinion. Ideas and intuition should come first as they are the feminine part and then the decision should be made from the male side, which analyzes, judges and streamlines. Whether we are talking about the external couple (husband and wife) or the internal couple (male and female parts of the Self) always remember that the outer Self is like the inner Self. Our external relationships are very similar to our internal relationships, if not exactly the same!

For example, when I started writing this book, I was first guided by my intuition for preparation, reading, training, research, tools and studying... Then I was again guided by my intuition to receive inspirational writings, here I'm talking about writing the first draft of each chapter. Sitting in front of each of the characters, I received the necessary information which I wrote out by hand in a *conscious* and un-*conscious* way... I did not always remember what I wrote and most of the time I thought that what I was writing was not okay. Then, after re-reading it, I noticed it was perfect. That is why I say that I sometimes write in an un-*conscious* way. I then wrote a second draft at the computer, but this time in a completely different way. I wrote more rationally this time, which allowed me to correct my mistakes and get a completely different point of view. I was open to receiving another perspective. To finalize the writing of this book, I used more of my masculine Self which is quite normal because this is the Self that puts things into action. I think every good work must consist of one part female energy (intuition and receiving) and one part male energy (action and giving). On the other hand, and we will look at it later, this relates more to the Arcanum "Temperance".

The Law, which is the perfect illustration of Love (The Lovers Arcanum) is the "Law of free choice in Love", this Law says that you have to be able to choose Love before anything else. You must be able to Love yourSelf before you can Love others, be able to please yourSelf before pleasing others and respect yourSelf in order to respect others.

At several points during our lifetime, we may find ourselves facing a crossroads. Any time we have to make a choice, for example: turn left or right... say Yes or No... choose White or Black. People tend to go right and follow everyone else. Going left is considered un-conventional, non-traditional. Therefore, we choose the "right", or the Easier way, right? We ask ourselves, "What would I look like? What would people say?"

The number 6 is not only related to sexuality, but also to marriage, associations, partnerships, unions, choices, decisions... and separations, illusory seductions, ambivalences, oppositions, in-decisions, hesitations, but what to choose? Too many choices. Confusion. Remember: confusion brings joy!

Once your choice is made there are still others to make. Everything has two sides; one is positive and one negative. There is a Luminous side and a dark side. In order to balance our energy we have to use both sides, rather like when we plug a lamp into an electrical outlet. For the Light to turn on there must be a perfect balance between positive and negative charges. To be complete and whole on our own is the ultimate goal. We do not have to look for "the person" who will make us complete, because we are fully complete by ourselves. This is because we are made in God's image. We are perfect and complete; no need to dominate or to be dominated anymore!

Sometimes in our dreams at night, our sub-*conscious* uses certain symbols to tell us about our Love life. Dreams help us balance our lives. For example, if you live with a lack of Love in the day time, your dreams will fix this offset. And that is true for any kind of lack, for instance, lack of affection in the daytime will be replaced by desserts in your dreams or in reality. The symbols are not necessarily sexual or clear. For me, I will often see a cousin or my Lover. They are symbols that I recognize as being related to my Love life, my emotional life. Unless I have a suitor that I do not yet know the existence of!

However, for example, to make me understand that I must make a choice in my daily life, my un-*conscious* will show me two possibilities such as two different meals: meat or fish. This kind of dream makes me understand that I have a choice to either satisfy my material Self or my spiritual Self in total communion with Life.

We *All* have the choice to choose God or the Devil, they are both creations and their purpose is for us to "learn". Neither one nor the other is the right choice. Whichever you choose will be the right choice. The selection is neither good nor bad, it is a choice. There are people who are here on Earth to experience God and others the Devil, so... who are we to judge? The night is necessary for leisure, in the same way that nature needs winter. We need daytime in order to live our experiences in a *conscious* reality... once more we must choose to live an *awakened* life, but is that your reality at the moment?

We always have the CHOICE and the CHOICE is ours!

Personal Applications

In this chapter, we are talking about the kind of person who experiences inner transformation through her feelings. This is someone who must make a choice; who must decide. She faces a crossroad. Will it be left or right? Yes or no? There are as many answers as there are questions... Several archetypes may be involved here: the great comprehensive, innovator and strategist, as well as the greatest manipulator, seducer, and house-of-cards builder ... This person uses the voice of "I", the voice of *consciousness*. Her main sensory mode will be visual. She acts out of pure dis-interest. She uses her energy to judge; judge others and their values. She is the greatest of sceptics. She is the type of person who suffers from a serious lack of optimism. She suffers from many problems with understanding, imagination, creation and innovation... if and of course only if, there are emotional blockages. Otherwise, a person who vibrates with positive energy will see things in an optimistic way. She will be interested, even fascinated. She will evolve in her spiritual life. Understanding, attention and concentration will lead her to the path of experimentation, imagination, innovation and creation. She understands. She is centered. She creates. She builds. She influences. She wants to speak. She holds. She fixes. Do you see what I am trying to illustrate?

To determine if there is an emotional blockage in your personal life, I suggest you take the time to answer the following questions honestly:

✓ **Do you experience dis-*interest* in your life?**

Are you a bored and dis-*interested* person?

If so, when do you experience dis-*interest*?

Is there something you can do to become more *interested*?

Is it dis-*interest* or rather the way you see the situation, the person or something else?

If you were watching the scene with more optimistic eyes, what would you see?

How we see things influences our perception of reality. Suppose you have access to two types of glasses. One pair gives you an optimistic view and the other a pessimistic view. Assign a colour to each pair of glasses. Then see a boring situation that you have experienced in the past, look at it using the glasses with the pessimistic view... and then using the optimistic ones... what do you notice? What are the differences? Now look at a future experience that might be boring and dis-*interesting*... but this time only look at the situation through the glasses with the optimistic tint. Thus, in the future, whenever you re-live an experience that is boring, look at it through the glasses with the optimistic tint!

✓ **Are you judgmental?**

Judging is like anything else, there are good and bad aspects to it. The judge is an archetype that may well be a visionary. He knows how to apply the Law... because he has the standards and rules at his finger tips and has very good judgment. It is very easy for him to decide. He knows what he wants, no one can fool him. On the other hand, the negative side of this archetype is called destructive criticism; used to put others down or for Self importance.

He judges without any compassion at all. He is hiding his true intentions. He may abuse his power and use his authority to manipulate others.

If you tend to judge, is it in a good or bad way?

If you judge negatively, why do you do this?

Do you need attention?

Do you need to be recognized?

Are you prepared to do anything to achieve your goal? Even manipulate others?

Remember: everything returns to the Source! The Source of *All*! What you transmit as energy today will come back tomorrow… So, be careful in your daily prayers!

✓ **Do you have trouble *understanding*? Are you "hard of hearing" as they say?**

If so, when do you have difficulty *understanding*?

What don't you *understand*?

According to the dictionary Antidote[1], one of the definitions attributed to the word *understand* is: "access the meaning of, discover".

If we change the word *understand* to discover…

When do you have difficultly discovering?

Is it different now?

If so, how is it different?

Does this relieve some weight or heaviness?

Is it easier for you to *understand* now?

---

1   Antidote is software that corrects and includes a French language dictionary

✓ **Do you have trouble using your *imagination*?**

If so, why are you blocking your *imagination*?

Do you tend to have headaches or migraines?

Yes! So, do not ask, you are probably blocking your vision from seeing with your third eye. Because *imagination* and vision are the same, if you refuse to receive or have refused to receive those images, you have created dis-ease. *Imagination* is a form of energy and, like any energy that is constantly blocked, it remains trapped... a form of crystallization. Yes! You have good reason to believe that *All* forms of physical illness are due to misplaced energy... so what are you waiting for, use your *imagination*? Think big! Really big!!!

✓ **If you have trouble imagining, then you probably have a hard time being *creative*. What would the *creative* process be without imagination?**

Have you ever had the opportunity to be *creative* in your life? For example: compose a text, draw a picture or create a totally new recipe...

Re-live an experience of *creativity*... What do you see? How do you feel? What do you hear? How are you? What are you thinking? What kind of emotion do you feel? What are your feelings? Bring that experience to your third eye between your two eyes... surround this experience in shades of blue indigo (purplish blue, very dark)... What do you see? How do you feel? What do you hear? How are you? What are you thinking? What kind of emotion are you experiencing? What are your feelings? Then bring that experience to your solar plexus located in the abdomen... surround this experience in a second layer of colour, a beautiful yellow hue (canary yellow). What do you see now? How do you feel now? What do you hear now? How are you? What are you thinking now? What kind of emotion are you living now? What are your feelings now? Next time you need to be *creative* and you are having difficulty, focus on your third eye and bring it *All* to your solar plexus. This way you will unite emotion and imagination, because the third eye is the seat of imagination and the solar plexus the seat of emotions.

✓ **Finally, if you have difficulty being imaginative and creative, you will probably find it difficult to *innovate*. What would an *invention* be without imagination and creativity?**

If you have difficulty being *innovative*, think of someone who is *innovative*. This person may be someone who is known for her *inventiveness* or simply someone you know who is *innovative*. Imagine you are that person... you are an *inventor*... you are creative... you have a lot of imagination... What are you experiencing? Enjoy the experience to the fullest while bringing with you what YOU need to stay *innovative*. Make a copy or a duplicate of the qualities you Love and want and bring them back with you. These *innovative* qualities are yours now. They are in you and now you can re-focus at any time and access these great re-Sources!

N.B: Lapis Lazuli is a beneficial stone that promotes *imagination, innovation and creativity*. Furthermore, it enables us to find the Source of our own physical and psychological problems and much, much more!

☆·.,.·´¯`·.,.¤ ~ ๑ °

Chapter 7

TRIUMPH

✈

The energy discussed in this chapter is an energy that is familiar to me. My life path is 7. This number is considered a sacred number and it emits a vibration of triumph and magical power. We are triumphant because we have finally chosen ourselves and victory over our internal conflicts. Our only purpose now is to reach perfection...

The "Law of Responsibility" is the Law corresponding to the Arcanum The Chariot which is the seventh Arcanum in tarot and associated with the seventh astrological house. This house corresponds to the others, which is normal since we have decided to choose ourselves first and then the others will come. This Arcanum says: " I am going forward on my life path", hence the link to the "Law of Responsibility". To move forward, standing t-All and mastering All parts of ourselves is the ultimate victory. It is a victory of the mind... of our mental part. To be *conscious* of whom we really are, to accept it and use it in a positive way. It is a combination of opposing forces. White and black make gray. It is neutrality; a balance. It is neither night nor day, but something in-between. An emptiness... it stops the mind. That is where everything is... *voilà*.

The Chariot is an Arcanum that mediates between Heaven and Earth. It is a messenger from God, Angels and Spirits. It is the fairy... the nature Angel... the nature child; the child that Loves animals, flowers, trees and the outdoors passionately. The Chariot represents a perfect balance between action and imagination; the perfection of God in human form. The human body is a vehicle that serves as a medium for communication between Heaven and Earth!

The man who fulfills his Divine Plan is now a complete being. He is a complete human being in perfect control of himSelf and able to accomplish his responsibilities. His human body is used to communicate the messages of Love he receives. Very often, when we are fulfilling our destiny we must do it alone… alone, but when we are whole, loneliness is not an issue. People are just passing through our lives. This is our life, not theirs… no one and nothing really belongs to us. We do not even belong to our own body, so no one else can belong to us either.

The perfect recipe is complete control of our feminine and masculine sides. We must be able to look at both sides of the coin and recognize what is positive and constructive on each side; just as with an electrical outlet you have positive and negative charges in the right proportion. We will then recognize that we are a medium for communication; an electrical body that vibrates and receives information, depending on the frequency we emit.

As I have explained before, my energy used to be more Yang, more masculine. I was a woman of action. To become a channel as I am now, I had to integrate more of my feminine side into my daily activities. I was not using it enough. First, I had to understand this and then I had to literally put aside my masculine side for a while to find a balance. During this period I started using more and more of my feminine side and my dreams at night were profoundly affected. One night, for example, I dreamed that my masculine side wanted my feminine side to die. Another night, I dreamed that I was making Love to mySelf. My male organ was very big compared to my female one. This illustrated the fact that my masculine side was still taking up a lot of space in my life.

The day I dreamed that I got married was when I understood that I had more control of mySelf. It meant that I had a union between my inner man and inner woman; between my Soul and inner God; between my different bodies, the physical one and the energetic ones. According to Jungian analysis, "the symbol of marriage is the process of individuation or integration of personality". I had managed to integrate *All* parts of my being. I had accepted my feminine and masculine sides as well as the negative parts of both. I had accepted *All* parts of mySelf; the Light as well as the Dark and could use them as allies. The dragons or demons within...

Shortly after, I went shopping as a real woman would. I made my wardrobe more feminine with high heels, skirts, dresses, blouses and I even bought several handbags. WOW! I fell like a woman[2] ♪♫♪. My body had changed. I was less in conflict with my mother. And my menstrual pain had also decreased. I learned to understand my emotions. Before, I had no emotion at *All*. Now I cry simply watching television. I can feel people miles away. Are they my emotions or yours? I am a medium of communication... and an Indigo child!

---

2   Referring to Shania Twain song

Personal Applications

In this chapter we are looking at the type of personality that has the ability to face the greatest challenges and bursts of strength. This is a person who knows her responsibilities. She follows her life path with pride. She Masters her inner demons. Several archetypes may be involved here: the Light worker, believer, sovereign as well as the biggest doubters, those who are blindly disciplined and dogmatic; working to negative ends. This person lives in the absence of Light, hates God and only believes in reason and separation, probably because of several experiences from past lives and also, perhaps, because of her values and culture and society, hence her identity. Doubt has also been created from her identity, because everything is profoundly linked... if and of course only if, there are emotional blockages. Otherwise, a person who vibrates in positive energy will feel *connected* to the Divine through higher channels. She will feel united to something larger, a link with the Celestial. She is inspired by *All* kinds of Divine energies. She can even see Light beings and feel them. She is happy, faithful and humble. (Yes, humble... I would like to comment here on HUMILITY; I believe that in spirituality everyone must remember to be humble, because humility is the ultimate quality to possess!) This kind of person can be felt for miles around, because she radiates her beautiful Light presence. She is united with God. She is. She believes. She knows. She is with God. She embraces life! And life smiles on her!

To determine if there is an emotional blockage in your personal life, I suggest you take the time to answer the following questions honestly:

✓ **Do you believe in *God*?**

If not, why?

Have you ever had a conflict with your father?

Have you ever had problems with an authority figure?

When did you stop believing in *God*?

In your opinion, is it necessary to believe in *God*?

Find the exact moment when you stopped believing in *God*; the moment you lost your FAITH. Ask for assistance to return to the very first time you stopped believing in him. Ask it aloud with your eyes closed and see the event... feel the event... hear what there is to hear... observe what happened at that time... Now, do you know why you do not believe in *God* anymore? Analyze the situation. Do you want to change anything? If so, what are the things you want to change? What is the first step you believe you can take to modify the situation so you can have faith again? Pretend you could make changes and see how time changes things... Remain in this state *All* the time necessary to incorporate the changes in you... Now, imagine yourSelf walking forward on your life path having faith in *God*. Have faith *God* is there for you! *God* is in you, because *All* re-Sources are in you!

✓ **Do you believe that reason is the only way?**

Have you ever experienced using your *intuition*?

I suggest you practice using your *intuition*. Several tools exist for this: the pendulum, reading tarot cards, automatic writing... First, train yourSelf using small, simple exercises like the following one. Take a coin and ask about something you have promised to do. Start with something small. For example: should I vacuum now or later? Then decide on the rules: yes = heads and no or later = tails. Flip the coin and see if you need to vacuum or not. Observe your reaction and how you feel about the answer you got. Was it the answer you wanted? If so, then you should now feel a vibration in you that calibrates the right way according to your Soul. This feeling is the frequency you must learn to recognize because it is the ONE you vibrate with when you are on the same level as your Soul. It means you are in tune with your *intuition*. Keep doing exercises like this and become an expert in recognizing when you are in tune with your *intuition*. You will no longer need to constantly act based on reason, since true direction is guided by *intuition*!

✓ **Do you believe in separation?**

From whom or what do you believe you are separated?

Look at the phenomenon of energy for example. Everything is made of energy. A person's energy resembles rays vibrating in unison. There are layers of energy around each of us and these layers also reflect other layers and so on. This illustrates very well that EVERYTHING around us, humans, animals, trees, plants, furniture and houses radiates energy and that the energy being radiated also emits energy. The image is analogous to the circles that form on the surface of water when we toss in a rock, or the way sound travels through the air in waves. Do you still believe in separation?

✓ **Do you tend to doubt?**

If so, when do you doubt?

Why do you doubt?

What does doubting mean to you?

What do you know beyond *All* doubts?

Doubting is much the same as lack of *confidence* or lack of *faith*, is it not?

"The Law of Faith is founded upon the recognition that we know more than we have read, heard, or studied;

we know more because we are more; we have a direct link to universal wisdom;

we only have to look, listen, and trust."

Dan Millman

What would happen if you continued on your life path knowing that you know more than anything you have read, heard or learned?

Remember, our energy is like water, we embrace everything... our personal and collective energy... our personal and collective *consciousness*... Furthermore, are we not channelling energy? Hence the link made by Dan Millman that we are *connected* to Universal Wisdom. Personally I think we must ask first, indicate our intention and pray or meditate. Then, *All* we have to do is look, listen and have *faith* that what we are requesting will eventually manifest at the right moment. The moment will be according to the Divine plan and not according to Tom, Dick or Harry!

✓ **Do you think you could be more en*light*ened?**

If so, I suggest a little introjections or introspection. Close your eyes and become *aware* of your inner flame, situated not far from your heart... See this beautiful flame... feel it... listen to what there is to hear... and stay in communion with your inner flame... Enjoy this beautiful moment... then spread the flame to every cell in your body... Imagine it running down to the tips of your toes, passing through your stomach, pelvis, legs, knees, calves, ankles, feet, through your chest, throat, neck, shoulders, arms, elbows, hands, fingers and finally from your neck to the top of your head... Imagine and feel the flame in *All* your being... in *All* your organs and in *All* your cells... You are illuminated... This flame Lights up from the inside out... When people see you they see and feel your Light... your "inner jewel"! Thus, whenever you feel the need, you just have to repeat this exercise to Light your inner flame.

✓ **She controls her inner dragons... Are you master of your inner dragons?**

The ultimate goal is to recognize them and know they are there but not to judge or favour one more than the other. It is important to go forward in complete control knowing you are right in the middle; too much is the same as not enough, so too white is like too black... too soft is no better than too hard. Behind every great misery hides our greatest discoveries and this is often where our gifts hide too. I highly recommend experiencing your miseries, knowing that in the end you will discover your greatest gifts of *All*! This is why we must get to know our inner demons!

Chapter 8

KARMA

According to several authors, the first seven tarot cards correspond to the Spirit and the following seven, to the Soul. The eighth Arcanum relates to Justice, but "Universal" Justice. The sword and scale illustrate this reality.

Under the energy of the number 8, which is represented by the symbol for infinity, we find initiatory tests and karma. This karmic Arcanum confronts us with our own words, thoughts and actions. What we have disseminated, we now collect. Here and now is the perfect moment for the harvest. Everything that happens is accurate. Anyway, whether we like it or not, Justice will be done based on what we created in the past, unless we forgive. The Lord taught us that the only Law that is superior to the "Law of Cause and Effect" is the "Law of Forgiveness".

People around often show us our karmas. They are there precisely because they vibrate at the same level as us, if I can express it this way. In other words, our frequency or vibration rate attracts precisely that kind of person to us. That is why sometimes when you meet people, there are some you are not attracted to at *All*, even some you know you really do not like. On the other hand, others emit a positive resonance towards you. Everything is energy: us, around us, the material, the *visible* and in-*visible*. Everything is made of energy. I really think that is why the "Law of Attraction" and the "Law of Vibration" work in concert. We attract what we vibrate, and the opposite is also true. Roses are red and violet are blue... believe it or not I Love you!

However, this chapter deals with a different Law called the "Law of Cause and Effect" or the "Law of Consequences". These are the effects or consequences of what we have thought, said or done. If our behaviour is Luminous, we will receive Light in return, but if our behaviour is dark, beware! There will certainly be a reaction!

Generally, in my dreams at night, I am informed about my behaviour through the symbol of a vehicle, among others. For example, my sub-*conscious* will use a colour for the vehicle shown to match my behaviour at that time... After analyzing one of my dreams I understood that my behaviour at the time was perfect. It was shown to me in the form of a white Cadillac. Wow! I hope this is also a predictive dream, because I want one! People who believe that a Cadillac doesn't fit with spirituality are way off base (are in the ditch (not on the right path)). In contrast, abundance is given to *All*. Abundance is, in fact, the result of the "Law of Attraction". So watch out...try to stay in the ball park. The ditches were created to help harvest.

White is the colour of Justice. It asks to be more detached because it is a sign of purity and to become more pure we must first detach ourselves. It is the colour associated, among others, with the Moon, the Virgin Mary and Artemis (Diane). The colour white is associated with great Luminous energy. It also reflects success and victory. In the end, I will get my white Cadillac!

This Arcanum makes us realize that everything happens for a reason. Nothing happens by pure coincidence. I looked at mySelf in the mirror one morning and, in a flash, saw my beloved cousin. Within a few hours, she was in touch with me. Another morning I had a red eye and, in a flash, saw my goddaughter. When I asked for news of her, I learned that she had a cataract and they made the diagnosis because she had a red eye! I dreamed that my cat had injured an eye. A few days later, I noticed that he had an infection in one eye. Eyes are windows on the Soul. Be careful... we can see your Soul and I see many lonely Souls!

I was guided to read about a healing technique practiced in the company of the beautiful Archangel Michael. Thanks again to my dreams, I learned about this technique which uses visualization to clean negative energy with a vacuum cleaner! I also dreamed my mother had bugs on her leg. Then a few days later, my mother told me she dreamed that her bathroom was full of bugs and that my late grandfather told her to clean them up with a vacuum cleaner. At that moment I understood why I had been guided to learn this technique. My dreams give me a lot of clues and I also receive information for others. What happens is always perfect; no need to justify or think, only listen to what you receive.

As I have already explained, the people around us are there because they vibrate, more or less, at the same frequency as us. This is called "resonance" in NLP or the mirror effect. When people talk and what they say creates a reaction in you, then it is the famous resonance effect. They are here in our lives to enable us to grow. They are part of our experience and _know_ledge. Our reaction is, in fact, this phenomenon called resonance. What we are seeing here is the great complicity of the "Law of Vibration" and the "Law of Consequences" working in unison. _All_ we have to do is remove the blindfold from our eyes in order to finally see that the reaction caused by something external is in fact an inner bug!

In Sanskrit the word karma means Returning... Returning to the Source! Yes! Our own inner Source located near the heart!

Personal Applications

In this chapter, we are discussing the energy that is related to someone facing Justice. This is not necessarily human Justice, rather Universal Justice. This person will have the opportunity to see her karmas and resolve them, if necessary. Wealth and abundance may also be part of her life since it is autumn, the harvest season. There may be several archetypes involved: the judge, lawyer, policeman, but also, the leader of a gang, smuggler, thief... If working in a negative way, this person will be powerless. She will experience a total lack of strength and vitality. She will live a deep im-balance. Her motivation will disappear and vanish along with her energy. She will experience financial, material and judicial problems. We are watching karmic cycles repeat themselves which is quite normal, since the person is completely blind... or un-*conscious*. Is she not blindfolded... of course only if, there are emotional blockages. Otherwise, a person who vibrates in positive energy will live in abundance and wealth and will be surrounded by material goods. She will be extremely strong. Strength and vitality are an integral part of her life. She is completely balanced. She plunges deeply into herSelf and is well centered. She takes her responsibility seriously and she perseveres. She is located in the GOLDen mean. She is fair and life gives back to her. How could it be otherwise? She radiates positive energy doesn't she?

To determine if there is an emotional blockage in your personal life, I suggest you take the time to answer the following questions honestly:

✓ **Do you live a life of *abundance* and *wealth*?**

Otherwise, when do you feel your life is impoverished and lacking in *abundance*?

What are your beliefs regarding *wealth* and *abundance*?

For example, I was asked once by a gentleman: "Chantal, are you not happy with your life as it is?" *All* because I bought a lottery ticket. We can easily hear the "limiting belief" of the gentleman in question: he believes that having millions would make him un-*happy*!

Wealth = un-*happiness*... this is a very limiting equation and the Universe and life do not want to hurt you in any way. If this is how you feel about money, life will make sure that you do not get millions. It protects you by listening to your requirements. This is also an example of the prayer: "Ask and you shall receive." I am talking about money here because it is the subject in question, but any other subject could be applied. Life, the Universe and your sub-*conscious* are here to protect you and fulfill your wishes! Once again, be careful what you wish for! And «pay» attention to your different beliefs, they are the center of your life!

✓ **Do you often have minor issues with the Law?**

Are you often caught speeding or parking illegally?

If speeding is the issue, then where else in your life are you going too fast?

Clearly, life chose to slow you down, but it is up to you to know where exactly you need to slow down in your life.

If you do not obey traffic rules, then, are there other rules in your life that you do not respect?

It is obvious that life is trying to make you realize that you do not respect rules, but you have to find the Source by yourSelf. Why are you dis*respect*ful?

If you park in no-parking zones, where are you currently parked in your life?

You are probably at the wrong place and life is trying to make you understand. It is a day sign. You know there are coincidences that are not coincidences!

Here is an example:

I was stopped for turning right on a red Light in Montreal. I live in Salaberry-de-Valleyfield, where, unless otherwise stated, we can turn right on a red Light. Coincidentally, I was wondering, exactly at that moment how my life was going and they gave me a ticket for over a hundred dollars because I turned right on a red instead of waiting for the Light to turn green. I acted instead of waiting for the right moment. I noticed today that at this point in my life, my personal year in numerology was 9. Yet, in our personal year 9, we are supposed to stop and think and wait the year out before starting new projects. I was not listening, I was acting! My question was answered rapidly. Thank you "Green Tara" for answering *All* my prayers so quickly!

✓ **Do you have the impression you are weaker?**

When do you or did you lose your *strength*?

The "hara" is in the center of the physical body and is the seat of *strength*. To harmonize this chakra, you can use the sound HOU or HUO. When chanting this mantra, visualize the colour of the chakra, which is yellowish orange, at the same time. When you are reciting the mantra HOU focus the sound on your "hara" located near the spine at the level of the navel (up to 2 finger widths above or below).

Harmonizing this chakra can be done through nourishment from the Earth, especially with foods that have absorbed a lot of sun. Expose yourSelf to the sun Light. Eat lots of yellow or orange coloured fruit and vegetables. Dress in yellow and orange colours, as well as medium blue. Drink water from a yellow or orange coloured glass or bottle that has been exposed to the sun for a few hours. Tai Chi and Qi Gong are physical exercises that can help you restore your entire initial *strength*. (Refer to: *Le livre des 28 chakras* see section on "hara", Élias Wolf.)

✓ **Do you feel that your *energy* has decreased?**

If so, when did you start losing *energy*?

In your opinion, why do you have less *energy*?

Do you remember the last time you felt full of *energy*?

What happened to make you slow down?

Do you have any physical problems?

Do you feel tired?

Do you still Love what you do?

Are you still passionate?

Is something making you sick or are you sick of what you do?

Yes! What are you waiting for to change? Make room for changes in your life, you are too resistant and experiencing a decrease in *energy*. Your reaction is normal, because what you are doing is done without Love. You should be listening to the voice of your heart and you are not. Start right now by trying to listen to the voice of your own heart? The only way that should be permitted!

✓ **Do you have many nightmares or recurring dreams?**

If so, what do you discern in your nightmares or dreams? Are there similarities? Are there differences?

Note the key element. Is there a link?

What is the general meaning of each of your dreams or nightmares?

The goal here is to understand what your sub-*conscious* is trying to tell you through your dreams. This type of dream will be repeated until you understand clearly. So look for over*All* meaning and the general direction of your dreams and not at specific details. You can use a symbolism dictionary for a guide, but first of *All* trust your instincts. We have *All* lived different experiences which is why each symbol may be interpreted differently. The symbolism of water brings me joy; I Love water, while for someone else, who may have nearly drowned, it could be traumatic. Go ahead, follow your feelings and *know*ledge and seek out what your Soul is trying to unveil!

Chapter 9

*KNOW*LEDGE
Ψ

THE Hermit is the archetype that vibrates under the influence of the "Law of *Know*ledge". This figure points out that it is time to stop and focus. Stop, rest and focus, so we can move better afterwards; a moment of necessary solitude. The Mystic, his cousin, is also reclusive, but for different reasons, spiritual ones, while Mr. Hermit lives in solitude for reasons that are not necessarily spiritual.

Anyone writing, reading, studying or doing research, for example, closely fits this archetype. In the game of Tarot, the Hermit is assigned the number 9 which is associated with the ninth astrological house and corresponds to superior education, University, traveling for long periods, spirituality and philosophy, hence the link with the "Law of *Know*ledge". In numerology the number 9 refers to the end of a cycle. At the end of a 9-year cycle, we start a new one. It is said that cats have nine lives! It is not recommended, according to numerology, to start a new project during your *personal year*[3] 9, since there is a good chance you may not get it finished! Instead, wait until year 1, a year of beginnings, re*new*al and spring... Beliefs... everything is beliefs, choose then with care!

Scholars, writers, poets, artists and anyone who needs time alone to think, create and communicate, even pray or meditate

---

3   To find out your personal year, you can calculate it like this:
     Example : if your birth date is January 5, 1949 and the current year is 2010,
     Then, 01/05/2010 = 0+1+0+5+2+0+1+0 = 9. Your personal year is 9.Example : if your birth date is July 31, 1989 and the current year is 2012,
     Then, 07/31/2012 = 0+7+3+1+2+0+1+2 = 16= 1+6 = 7. Your personal year will be 7 in 2012.

are considered Hermits. This reminds me of the image of an old, wise man; my grandfather and my godfather. For a long time, I attributed this wisdom to age but I now know that I also have this wisdom inside me. We *All* have seeds of wisdom within us. We are already at several incarnations, so it is normal that we carry some wisdom in our luggage; luggage full of experience and *know*ledge. My godmother is also an image of wisdom... my grandmother... She has shown me that I have inherited this great quality. Alberto Villoldo illustrates it in his book: *Shaman, healer, sage*, when invoking the sacred space...

"To the winds of the North.
Hummingbird, Grandmothers and Grandfathers,
Ancient Ones
Come and warm your hands by our fires
Whisper to us in the wind
We honor you have come before us,
And you will come after us, our children's children..."

My grandmother showed me in my dreams that I kept this beautiful quality by invoking the symbol of two bags of Clementine's on the kitchen table. Orange is the colour that relates to the spirit of holiness and the sacral chakra: creativity, procreation and sexuality. When we dream of fruit at night, it is an indication of our emotional life and abundance; abundance of *know*ledge... Furthermore, in Feng Shui, the northeast is the place to integrate *know*ledge. Be sure to put a library filled with books on that side of your house and see what you will integrate.

This energy is an energy that vibrates in *All* the cells of my body; an energy that vibrates within me. I think we have to be a Hermit sometimes when we study, write and work on our inner being. We work on our inner world to feel better inside and not be influenced by the outside world. When *All* is well with us... alone... and then, if anything comes to us from outside, something extra, then *All* the best and thank you God!

With a Light in his hand, this old wise man thinks about the days to come. His purpose may be en*light*enment, but the Light must stay inside, because it is useless to blind those who are not supposed to see it... En*light*enment is suitable for his cousin the Mystic and the Alchemist. The Magician and the Alchemist are cousins, however the Magician is more centered on the tools that help bring what he wants to life; human potential. He has that power. The Alchemist, meanwhile, focuses on his spiritual strengths. He studies and practices the "Universal Laws". At least I hope so! En*light*enment is the similarity between the Alchemist and the Mystic; both evolve at the level of the spiritual transformation of the being.

Often, while meditating I see mySelf in other lives. Once, I saw mySelf in the year 1300 and I was a man sitting at a table with a candle, as I do now, writing, studying, doing research and development and decoding mysteries. A long time ago, I was a scholar and writer... Today, I understand my tastes, interests, gifts and talents, in my current life in 2013. I have done a lot of research and development, over time, in chemistry laboratories and I still do some now in my office, but in a different way. I have been analyzing my dreams every day for several years now. I have been studying since the age of 5. I have read thousands of books and intend to write several books and create tools for spiritual development. That is why I identify mySelf with scientists, artists, science, research and development.

That is how, in this life, I came to study, develop and write about my own abilities and *know*ledge and also my *know*ledge of human beings. When I was younger, I knew in my heart, that we know much more than we think we know. In short, I knew there was a way to gain access to information and *know*ledge. It is as if we were a sports car driving our whole life on cruise control at only 50 km/h... what a waste!

Like St-Francis, my destiny is to communicate with animals, nature and do some healing work. Like him, I help people discover their vocation, career or life mission. Like him, I am sensitive to the environment. Earth, our dearly beloved mother is going to be angry very soon!

Solitude helps us to remember but sometimes it is not necessary to remember everything! Our body shows this because when we experience a great trauma, it ensures that we forget. So is it really necessary to remember everything? Probably not, otherwise we would remember wouldn't we?

Personal Applications

In this chapter, we are referring to a person who should take a break to rest and think. The goal could be to become more *know*ledgeable or to find a new direction. Whatever the case, it is important to stop; we cannot always be in motion. We must find a balance... This type of person may lack *awareness*. She could be un-*generous*. She could also experience in-*ability*, anxiety and concern. Her impotence could give rise to her lack of Self confidence. We could be dealing with a loser. This type of person can also be compared to a shark because she only works to win and at the expense of others who becomes losers... if and of course only if, there are emotional blockages. Otherwise, a person vibrating positive energy will live in happiness, joy and completeness. She has great confidence in herSelf. This person is extremely generous and has an almost contagious magnanimity. She has great strength for creativity and manifestation. She trusts. She trusts life in general. She remains true to herSelf. She desires. She manifests. She deserves. She believes in herSelf. And luck is on her side! She works according to the win-win dolphin strategy!

To determine if there an emotional blockage in your personal life, I suggest you take the time to answer the following questions honestly:

✓ **Are you lacking *Self* confidence?**

Why do you think this is so?

What do you not trust about yourSelf?

How long have you been like this?

On a scale of 1 to 10, how would you rate your *Self confidence*?

Focus on your "kalpa taru" chakra which is located in the upper abdomen just below your chest. Visualize a beautiful green grass colour. Imagine vitality, hope and health. Your chakra should turn clockwise at the frequency it is supposed to turn... Feel each turn and feel your *Self-confidence* increasing... Stay in this state, visualizing your chakra for some time and, when you feel that your *confidence* level is where you would like it to be, proceed to the next step. Now, kneel down and pretend to be a cat. Tilt your head and your upper body as if you were bowing, then lift your body and round your back like a cat's. Do these exercises at least three times. On a scale of 1 to 10, how would you rate your *Self-confidence* now?

Repeat until your rating is at least 7 out of 10.

✓ **Do you always lose or *win*?**

Either case is not good. There is no middle ground here.

If you often lose, then what is it you are unable to achieve?

If you are usually the *winner* over others, then what is it you are unable to achieve without taking something from another person?

In either case, the person does not feel able to reach his goal. The *winner* thinks he can reach it, but he cannot do it without harming others, so he is unable to do it alone.

What is currently missing in your life that makes you unable to achieve your goal without taking something away from someone else?

What is the first good step you could take today to achieve your goal without taking something away from someone else?

✓ **Are you un-*generous*?**

If so, when are you stingy?

Have you ever been a *generous* person in your life?

If so, how have you changed?

What are the emotional, mental and environmental differences?

Is it possible for you to restore your character from that time?

Pretend you are that person again... what is happening? How do you feel? What do you see? What do you hear? What are people saying around you? What are they saying about your great *generosity*? Enjoy and savour this great moment intensely in *All* its details of indulgence and kindness. Imprint the beautiful qualities of your *generosity* on *All* the cells of your body and your Soul. You have a kind Soul. Note how your Soul makes you feel about this beautiful energy. You are at ONE with *All* parts of your being and you vibrate in harmony with your Soul. The Game of life is to give and receive and your Soul knows this. When you are in this great mode of *generosity*, your soul vibrates intense joy, so feel what it wants to communicate to you! Now, I suggest you honour this beautiful experience by giving it a name, colour, emotion, symbol - it does not matter how - the intention here is to honour the experience of *generosity* as you understand it!

✓ **Do you worry a lot?**

If so, what are you worried about?

In your present life what are you missing that might make things *calmer* and more *serene*?

What is causing you so much worry?

And suppose that what is currently happening in your life is really how it was meant to be... As if it had *All* been planned for many years... As if, no matter what you do, it would not affect this destiny. That is the way it was designed and you cannot change anything except your own perception of reality! Stop worrying about everything and anything at *All*, because you are feeding on a Source of energy that, over time, will produce some strange effects on you, believe me.

Now, knowing this, how do you feel?

Are you still as worried?

If so, re-focus by saying that anxiety is an emotion not centered on Love. Then, re-focus on Love as energy...

You can do this re-focusing with any type of emotion that is not beneficial for you and it works fine. You only have to think about it and you will re-focus immediately!

✓ **Do you ever feel *power*less?**

If so, does it happen often?

When do you feel *power*less?

Can you relate your *power*lessness to a lack of re-Sources or strength?

If you think it is due to a lack of re-Sources, what are they? In other words, what do you think you are missing in your life right now that would make you feel more *powerful*?

How could you find the missing tools?

Like everyone else, you have already experienced *power*. Analyze a situation when you felt *powerful* and take note of the tools you had. Then, consider what you need now, in your life, as tools to feel *powerful*. What do you notice? You can now recognize the missing tools and you can access them again. If they are yours by Divine right, there is no possible separation. By recovering these tools and you know exactly how to re-integrate them into your life today, you will feel a new energy of great *power*... if and only if... you really want it. After *All*, you are made in the image of God which is, in my opinion, the greatest *power* of *All*!

Chapter 10

CYCLES

The 'Law of Cycles" is the law referred to in this chapter. Seasons, the ebb and flow of waterways, night and day, life and death are *All* examples of cycles. Progress is continual... Change is constant... Spring seeding, summer fiestas, fall harvest and winter rest. The "Law of Cycles" or the "Law of Returns" means eternal returns and constant re*new*als...

I awake up. I am thirsty. I drink water. Water cleanses, purifies and re-balances... There is no distinction between my body and my house. My body and temple is the vehicle of my Soul... The alarm clock rings to wake me up. It is an alarm that indicates the need to make a decision - the need to decide on a direction - the need to wake up and live *consciously*. An un-expected event, like so many others, sensitizes me and I will act in a way I never imagined I would... I pray and ask. I ask to be a "waitress of Love" and am sent Love. I ask to serve food and am given food. WOW!

The "Law of Cycles" reminds us that we must become the centered observer. It's so easy to lose our way. We turn and turn and lose North. We become dizzy because there is too much to do or we take on too much? In Tarot, we associate this kind of energy with the Wheel of Fortune. This Arcanum shows us the major strength of fight or fusion which we *All* face at some time in our existence. This beautiful Wheel turns and puts us, or re-places us in front of the different cycles of life; it puts us back where we belong... The significance of the Wheel refers to both the end and the beginning. The Wheel illustrates the ups and downs we face when we come home.

The Wheel of Fortune, the tenth tarot Arcanum, is associated with the tenth astrological house that represents career, social success, and mother... our similarities with her. What we inherited from her, not only our inner motherhood... but also fatherhood; our inheritance... inner and outer.

When I took my courses in Tarot, I had to sleep with each card for five nights. That's why I talk about my dreams so often. When I slept with the card for the Wheel of Fortune, I dreamed about my career and professional life and what they would be in the future... I saw that, although I will be recognized and made popular through many kinds of media, I will remain very humble. I also dreamed that I would be an innovator in the elaboration of new metaphysical, esoteric, theoretical and practical techniques and methods. Furthermore, I dreamed that I would develop my senses to a higher level and take a fall (hence the ups and downs of the "Law of Cycles") but would easily land on my own two feet... It will be simple for me then to continue my path and the gains will be much easier. This metamorphosis is essential for further communication with the in-*visible* world.

Studying this Arcanum helped me understand many things. First, I am truly *connected* to the other world; the in-*visible* world and its energy. Even at night sometimes, I live in a state of *consciousness* and receive lots of information. Answers to questions I ask mySelf or other information necessary for my development and healing. It is much clearer now than before...

The energy that emanates from the "Law of Cycles" and the Wheel of Fortune shows us, if we really want to see it, what we bring with us from past lives: our luggage and heritance. In my course of humanist hypnosis, in October 2007, I experienced something very special. That week of training made me *aware* of the famous phenomenon of "resonance" in every fibre of my being; material and energetic. In hindsight, I am convinced that this training was ONE of the biggest triggers for my *awakening*. Olivier Lockert, President of the French Institute of Hypnosis and a humanist hypnosis trainer, was talking about some cases he had seen and I felt as if he was talking about me... He was talking about being crazy. I know in a previous life I had a mental illness and then, because of what he was saying, my Soul vibrated, hence the phenomenon of resonance. Recognition was accomplished... Moreover, in this life, I was afraid of mental illness. I experienced some strange things that led me to question mySelf. It is said that often those who are schizophrenic, for example, are people who have achieved a high level of intelligence. They are afraid and WHAM! They become puppets as if the wires were cut and OOPS, there is no one at home; only puppets. Then during the training we had to do an exercise to help us to go into the Matrix, but I was afraid, so I did not do it. One night, during this training, I wrote an affirmation on a piece of paper that I put on my bedside table. I wanted to receive the information necessary to do the exercise without being afraid, because I was afraid of mental illness. In my dream that night, I was walking on a road calmly and suddenly I fell in a hole; into emptiness. There was a hole in the road and I fell in. Without panicking, I raised my arm to signal my presence, that was *All*. I raised my left arm in which I held a little pink purse. Following this dream, I did the exercise alone and I went into the Matrix. My feet were spinning like a carousel, but I did not panic. Instead, I stayed calm and experienced the "present moment"... without fear. Remember, there are only two types of emotion, according to the teachings of Jesus: Love and fear. And fear is the opposite of Love. Fear is lack of Love! The trick is always to re-center yourSelf on the energy of Love and you will have it *All*!

Studying this card also allowed me to see my various gifts and talents: clairvoyance, hyper-sensitivity, channelling, mediumship, healing, metaphysics (studies, prayers, affirmations...), research and development (analytical sight) and especially my great ability to intuitively understand my dreams. Cycles show us our various talents, strengths and weaknesses... but even if they are strengths or weaknesses we still repeat them, unless of course, we correct them! It is like a nightmare: as long as you do not understand, you repeat the same dream or nightmare. Everything depends on how you choose to see the situation! Such are the numerous cycles of life!

Personal Applications

In this chapter, we are talking about a person who experiences a happy or sad event and obeys the "Law of Cycles". The "Law of Cycles" demonstrates a form of repetition necessary for our evolution. Good or bad repetition, but still repetition. Healing begins with *awareness* of this repetition, because it creates great understanding. This fabulous understanding corrects what has to be corrected for the generations to come, so what is keeping you from becoming *aware* of the phenomenon of repetition in your life? Heal to improve the lives of future generations. This is a great repetition we can pass on as an inheritance! A person who evolves in negative energy will focus on Ego-centrism. She will have narcissistic tendencies. We might believe that she is absent, dull, in-sensitive, or even lost. She will be very lonely and isolated as well. Such a person will often have panic attacks. She is very agitated and angry and experiences dis-respect and condemnation... if and of course only if, there are emotional blockages. Otherwise, a person vibrating positive energy will live in peace and humility. She will be at the level of BEING. This kind of person is extremely present and she will experience an *awakening*. Her gifts will become clear and she will use an un-conventional form of telepathy; the voice of her inner guide. Compassion, grace and freedom are some of her values. Finally, silence is golden! She bows. She is. She respects. She embodies. She finally becomes the centred-observer on her own path!

To determine if there is an emotional blockage in your personal life, I suggest you take the time to answer the following questions honestly:

✓ **Do you think you are an Ego-centric person?**

If so, when are you Ego-centric?

Have you ever had an experience during which you were more *altruistic* or more *human*?

The thymus chakra is what we are dealing with here. It is located above the heart chakra about halfway between the heart and the throat. Its colour is a beautiful turquoise. The thymus gland is considered the seat of the Soul in the physical body during incarnation. When we are Ego-centric, we are no longer ONE with our Soul. The Ego feels separated. It thinks it can live alone. It thinks it is a unique and single entity. At the same time, the Ego is the part of us that imagines everything which produces negative emotion. Our Ego is the creator of our own horror scenes. So what can you do today to control the part of yourSelf that separates you from the rest of *humanity*?

I will give you a little trick that will help you recognize the work of your Ego. Any emotion or feeling you may have other than Love is a strategy from your little friend, if we can call it that. Once you become *aware* of this, trust your inner guide for the rest…

✓ **Are you addicted to drugs or cigarettes?**

If so, then you probably have a blockage at the level of the thymus chakra. This chakra is the seat of the Soul in the physical body during incarnation, as I mentioned earlier, and it is also the seat of the "Divine Self" where the "Divine flame" is found. If you deny your Divine Self or if you have committed wrongs or crimes against humanity for example, that would explains why your chakra is not working well. You take refuge in some form of addiction such as tobacco or marijuana (see the book: *Le Livre Des 28 Chakras de*

Élias Wolf p.142 and 143) to escape reality! If any evidence shows that your chakra is not functioning as it should... you are dis-*connected* from your Soul!

✓ **Do you think of yourSelf as absent?**

If so, when are you absent?

Do you believe you are *incarnated*?

If so, what is your *incarnation*?

Have you ever felt that you were *present*?

Yes! When? Why?

What is preventing you from being *present* here and now?

When we are absent, we are dissociated from our own physical body; we are elsewhere. We are not in the "*PRESENT*". Living in the *present* is, in fact, the secret to "HAPPINESS". That's why it's called *present*... By living in the *present* we do not experience any problems since, generally speaking, problems belong in the past or the future. We can manage to push the problem, emotion; stress... into the future and in the end, there is often no problem at *All*. Is it because we did not nourish the negative thoughts or is it some other phenomenon? Probably, whatever happens, the result is positive. I will illustrate this theory with a personal example. When my Aunt Marie died, a few years ago, I had to read a text from the bible in front of everyone in church. I deeply Loved my Aunt; I was grieved and had to perform. I then delayed my stress until that day. Then, on the day, I delayed my stress until the last minute. Then, what I knew was that I was in front of the church reading the text exactly the way I imagined I would. Conclusion: I did not experience any stress that day; neither before, nor during. I remained focused on the *present* that's *All*. Furthermore, I no longer feel stressed anymore about the future, because that day I was successful!

N.B.   Aunt Marie was one of my Guides! I say was, because she is not anymore. She was beside me until Jesus took over, or rather until I allowed Jesus to take over...

I saw her beside me in a dream until I crossed over into a new stage of my life and at that point she did not cross with me. At the other end of the tunnel, there were five or six people waiting for me *All* dressed in long robes or tunics. The only one I really recognized was Jesus. That is how I know she is no longer with me... as a Guide at least.

✓ **Do you tend to isolate yourSelf?**

If so, why?

Are you afraid? Of what are you afraid?

Do you feel abused? How have you been abused?

Do you protect yourSelf? From what are you protecting yourSelf?

Do you have trouble getting along with others?

What are you hiding?

What are you afraid to reveal?

Have you been hurt in the past and now you keep a distance?

How can you open up to others?

How can you change the beliefs that limit and distance you from others?

Imagine you can *open yourSelf* up to others... what happens when you do this? What do you see? What do you hear? What do you feel? Explore the beliefs that you have when you are *open to others*... Write down those beliefs... Now, what can you do to keep those beliefs in the present so you can be more *open to others* from now on?

✓ **Have you ever experienced telepathy?**

When your thymus chakra is functioning as it should, you are able to communicate with other beings via telepathy. However, we are talking about un-conventional telepathy. Let me give you an example of telepathy. One evening, I was in the bathroom. Note that, for me, the bathroom is a place where I receive a lot of information, probably because of the great amount of water centered there. I heard a friend talking to me. We talked for several minutes. I have no doubt that this experience was telepathy, because I heard her voice and I did not have time to finish my sentences before she started answering me. She had her own personality and her own way of answering my questions; something my imagination could not have imitated. We actually had a Soul to Soul conversation.

Chapter 11

FROM "EGO" TO "EQUAL"
=

This chapter will discuss energy, strength and Power. The lion's aggressive strength is juxtaposed to the image of the spiritual strength of the Virgin Mary. This is a fight that turns into a victory; the victory of the Spirit world over the "MATERIAL" world. Not destruction caused by Mr. "Ego", but triumph of the inner Self, the Divine part of the being: Triumph over illusion, suffering and fear, created by Mr. "Ego". This entity that feels separated but believes it *possesses* power and control. To possess or be possessed, that is the question.

That night, I experienced "healing", as if I was healing... as if, by the act of healing, YOU would also be healed. I saw a Light; a dazzling white Light and also a green ONE... Mercy, wisdom, wealth, victory, hope, healing and a new spring were blooming. Subsequently, I found mySelf lying on the grass next to my grandfather; my late grandfather... I felt an ending; the end of his protection, because I now have the great Power which is Love, the greatest Power of *All*. I have the strength of the Virgin mother Mary, our feminine side. I am finally cured, or at least in the process of healing.

In tarot, the eleventh Arcanum is called Strength... This Arcanum is associated with the eleventh house in astrology, which means aspirations, friends, and membership in a system. Often, to learn more about an Arcanum, we can look at the three cards that come before and the three cards that follow. The evolution of before and after... Here, we can see that Justice originates in Strength, thus karmas, the "Law of

Cause and Effect" - the "Law of Consequences" and it leads to... Temperance, neutrality and purification... the "Law of inner transformation by cleansing darkness at the un-*conscious* level". Moreover, if we do the theosophical calculation for the number 11, we obtain 2 (1+1=2): The Female Pope, dualities, dreams, clairvoyance and Spirituality.

This energy warns us not to become like Icarus, the mythological character who represents the values of the Soul centered on human Love and forgets that the only true and eternal Love is based on Divine Love. God is the Source; the Divine Source and internal fountain of youth, the Source of Light. Light is Love and *know*ledge and it is part of our Being! At least you can channel it if you want...

Life is an enormous school. We are here to learn. We *All* have different karmic lessons to learn. We talked about the lion, the male Self, ferocious, aggressive and protective and also about the energy of the Virgin Mary, the female Self, gentle and Divine. When the lion takes too much space in our lives, it somehow takes away from the capabilities, potential and values of our inner female. She then suffers from an inferiority complex... hence the battle, the struggle within us. "Our worst enemies are within us", says the Lord. David and Goliath are both within us. The lion dominates and the Virgin Mary is purity. The symbolism represented by the Arcanum Strength in tarot is for finally achieving purity of mind and innocence; the innocence of a child. This means our inner child, the child we *All* have within us. The only ONE that really belongs to us and, again, does he really belong to us?

An image comes to my mind. Like a flash... I am riding a horse alongside some other girls, cats and dogs. This illustrates my strength. I am moving forward on my life path by becoming *aware* of what is un-*conscious* and gradually, with time, bringing it into *consciousness*. This is a form of healing. Bringing to *consciousness* leads to healing... Now I know, therefore I see. And now I correct it when I see it; and I re-correct it again and again until it completely disappears... This is the healing process. This image also shows me my various gifts: healing, clairvoyance, channelling, mediumship... Then I move forward on my life path with my Guides and I am also a Guide when it's meant to be.

"I master my emotions and express them calmly and serenely" is a positive affirmation that anyone can use under the influence of the Strength Arcanum. In numerology, 11 is a number of higher vibrations. It represents excess, intemperance, overflow, violence, exaggerated judgment, if in a negative vortex. Yes, the energy of 11 is similar to that of the Virgin Mary, but it can also be found under the guise of the greatest of rebels. On the other hand, remember that the archetype of the rebel is a key element in human development. Having made a lot of progress in that direction, he is an invaluable help to everything that touches on human enrichment far and near.

Control and domination are the principal characteristics of the Arcanum, Strength. Who is dominating and controlling whom? One day I went horseback riding at Mont Tremblant. I had the good luck, even if luck does not exist, to practice this wonderful sport on the back of a beautiful horse named "Apollo". It was the first time I had gone horseback riding. As a child, I had ridden ponies but never a horse. At least not in this lifetime... Apollo showed me that Love is everything. I did not use a whip or even dig in my heels as my guide suggested. Instead, Apollo listened to me; I patted him, talked to him and Loved him. We were on the same wavelength, in synchronisation together.

Later I mentioned this to one of my clients in my office and he told me that normally it takes several years to have a relationship like that with a horse. He has one himSelf and he does not have this kind of relationship with the horse. I have experienced the same thing with "Nestley" the cat. We humans have, in most cases, a tendency to respond to violence with violence. Nestley used to bite a lot. For him it was a game and when we responded with a slap he would come back with a second bite. This was an ongoing game between us. So, one day, I had a brilliant idea to answer with a kiss on the top of his head. I noted with great pleasure, that he stopped biting. In fact these two examples illustrate perfectly that we must first give Love in order to receive it! Love heals everything! The Virgin Mary's energy represents the side of us that is made of pure Love, gentleness and kindness... our feminine side. Thank you Apollo for opening my third eye!

Strength is governed by the "Law of Absolute Effort". We need to spend time learning. We must make the effort to become Masters of our emotions and be able to express them peacefully and quietly. Peace of mind. No matter how fast we live our life path, we must put some effort into transcending the material and living within the Universal Laws in neutrality and "equality". We are *All* "equal"! So, let go of your Ego...

Personal Applications

In this chapter, we are referring to the type of person who lives events that will possibly generate inner struggles. On her journey, she may have moments of great pain, struggle and other events that will enable her to improve her personality and make her much stronger each time... Several archetypes may be involved here: the visionary, inventor, great thinker but also the eccentric, strange bird, dreamer. A person who vibrates negative energy will tend to run out of ideas and structure. She will be narrow-minded. She will be dys-*harmonious* internally and externally, because it amounts to the same thing. She cannot feel anything, otherwise she will be destroyed! This, of course, is only the case, if there is an emotional blockage. Otherwise, a person vibrating positive energy will live according to the voice of her muse and intuition. She will have a great sense of aesthetics. Her inspiration, creativity and visionary capacity will be fully developed because she lives in total harmony. She hears. She sees. She is creative. She is inspired. She has wings. Wings on her back or her feet depending on the kind of strange bird she is!

To determine if there is an emotional blockage in your personal life, I suggest you take the time to answer the following questions honestly:

✓ **Do you tend to run out of *ideas*?**

If so, do you know someone who is always full of *ideas*?

Describe this person... write down everything that comes to mind when thinking about this person. What do you hear... what do you see... what do you think she feels? Take the time to write down everything that comes to your mind when thinking about this person, because next time you run out of ideas, use this person has a model!

I would also like to add a comment here. Did you know that, when you describe someone, the description you give is partly of yourSelf? What you see are YOUR QUALITIES in others! You are just like that person you know who does not run out of *ideas*! This is the mirror effect...

✓ **Are you missing *structure* in your life?**

If so, where are you missing *structure*?

Have you ever been *structured*?

Why aren't you *structured* at present?

Do you think it is always good to be *structured*?

Remember a time in which you were very well *structured*... see yourSelf at that time. What do you see? What do you hear? What do you feel? Take note of that experience of *structure*... the characteristics... atmosphere... environment... time period... people who shared your life... and activities... Write down everything you remember... Now take a look at your life and note the differences... What is different? What do you notice? In Light of those differences, how can you bring more *structure* to your life right here and now?

✓ **Are you narrow minded?**

If so, when do you think you are narrow minded?

Have you ever had to be more *open minded*?

Have you ever experienced letting go of your own ideas, beliefs, and values and submitting, in total confidence, to what was happening at that time?

A child is the perfect embodiment of innocence, purity and amazement. He is constantly in a state of *open-mindedness*. He lives as if he knew absolutely nothing... and is always looking for discoveries, newness and beauty. Tell me about your relationship with your inner child. What type of inner child do you have? Are you a Divine child, nature child, wounded child, orphan child, eternal child, magical child or innocent child? (To learn more about the different archetypes of the inner child see Caroline Myss's book entitled *Sacred Contracts*). One thing is certain, if you are narrow minded, your inner child does not truly speak unless he is wounded or abandoned...

I propose that you find a comfortable sitting position with your eyes closed and ask to be re-*connected* to your inner child... Learn to recognize this child who really needs you and ask him questions... Wait for an answer... the answer could be an emotion, picture, sound, intuition, symbol... The type of question might be: what type of inner child do I have? Is he/she a Divine, nature, wounded, orphan, eternal, magical or innocent child? When you have an answer, continue asking questions... The aim is to *awaken* the child you have forgotten. When you are finished asking your questions, ask him to stay close to you and that way you will take the good qualities of your inner child! Qualities that you have had but have forgotten!

✓ **Do you sometimes experience dys-*harmony*?**

If so, when?

The chakra related to *harmony* is at the back of the head. When this chakra is un-balanced you may experience some inner dys-*harmony*. You will need to re-balance it. To do so, I suggest you imagine gold coloured meridian points, starting at the level of your heart and going up to the chakra at the back of your head. Then, imagine other meridian points starting from your third eye chakra up to the chakra at the back of your head. These meridian points are always a gold coloured hue. Visualize the energy passing through the channels you have just built. The energy leaving from the heart is green and the one leaving from the third eye is indigo (a dark blue-purple hue). And when you have brought the green and indigo energy to the back of the head chakra, visualize the middle of the back of your head, coloured in a shade of ice blue (pale blue-grey). Do these exercises three times and repeat them every day, as needed. No more than three times a day and not exceeding three weeks in a row.

✓ **Tell me what song comes to your mind these days?**

The songs that come to your mind in your daily life are either the answer to ONE of your questions or a link to a memory or, if a song frequently recurs in your mind, it may be the song of your Soul. Each Soul has its own song. Everyday we thank Father Sun for being able to sing the song of life when we open the sacred space... The chakra at the back of the head is the chakra of choice for anyone whose primary sense is hearing. When I ask you what the song is that comes into your mind right now, your Soul is giving you a sign. It is up to you to discover the hidden message behind this song... you can proceed this way with the help of Spirits, Angels, Archangels and Guides and thereby practice your clairvoyance! Furthermore, you can do this for inspiration and creativity. I hope that the Arcanum, Strength, will be with you and your SPIRIT and not with your Ego!

☆·.,.·´¯`·.,.¤ ~ ๑ °

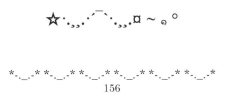

Chapter 12

THE MISSION, THE LIFE PATH
.·´¯`·.,><(((((°> <°))))><.·´¯`·.

We often talk about voluntary sacrifices. Yes, voluntary sacrifices for a belief, idea or life mission; as Christ so well demonstrated. In tarot, the card related to sacrifice is The Hanging Man; the Twelfth Arcanum of the game. It is also associated with the twelfth astrological house where the sign of the zodiac, Pisces, resides. If the fish of your dreams is big enough it may represent the "preachers" or Christ, a spiritual Master... another link with the Saviour. He is the preacher and we are the fish!

The Saviour, the Messiah, the victim; *All* imaginable archetypes representing the energy of The Hanging Man. *All* these characters have something in common; sacrifice! But are they really *conscious* of it? The twelfth astrological house is the house of the un-*conscious* and family shadows. Un-*consciousness*, shadows, night and moon; turn on the Light it is very dark here, I am afraid!

That night I spent the night healing... and finding solutions for the future. I saw a lot of colours... if I allow *All* the colours of life into my life, I will strengthen my integrity. What an idea! And it is My idea. May I speak a little bit with the geniuses of this world? You think it is your idea. Well I have some news for you. You have just channelled an idea floating around you. Since everything is energy... ideas are energy too. But you have a lot of nerve claiming the idea is yours. You do not impress me as geniuses, but let's move on.

In tarot, The Hanging Man is associated with people having a *connection* with the Divine, those who are carrying out their life mission, and those who let go easily... That is why we refer to voluntary sacrifice; to accomplish a life mission demands some sacrifice. You must have faith that what you are doing is the best choice possible. We have to trust that God is our Source and he will give us *All* we need and even more: the different colours of life, the rainbow, a visible link, for a moment, between Sky and Earth, communication between God and me, communication between Souls, you and me, my life mission. I am a rainbow... and you?

Currently, my life mission is, among others, to transmit what I receive, to guide and *awaken* my brothers and sisters with whom I have the privilege to share a part of the path. And it can even be done simply through inspiration... I am on a trip here on Earth, just like you, to learn and teach what I learn... But a lot of people are afraid to be alone; they are afraid of silence... Sitting at the edge of the water, I see some bugs, half black and half white and I see them changing colour before my eyes. They become green... emerald green. The Yin Yang balance, health... Transformations heal our internal bugs. Don't they say that the world was created out of chaos? Don't we have to break eggs to make an omelette? When I experience negative energy, I am not necessarily talking about negative thoughts or words, but rather a lack of sleep, for example. I am un-balanced and a little dis-oriented. Once I am calmed down, relaxed and in balance, I find *All* my possibilities, *All* my abilities. I have experienced this several times. Before, I did not necessarily understand it, but now I am *aware* of what is happening. I am in the kitchen walk-in. I am looking for a cover that goes on one of my dishes. I feel im-patient and am looking and looking in vain. I am *conscious* of my state; a state that cuts me off from the rest of the Universe, a state that cuts off my inner communication. Then I calm down and focus. I ask for help to find the cover and in a short period of time, I turn around and see it right next to me.

Sacrifice, sub-mission and being a victim are *All* possible facets evoking the twelfth Arcanum of the tarot. We might submit to someone else, we may also submit to our Ego. When the Ego has control, we can feel like a victim or a servant... At the service of the Soul and not of the Ego. Anger, bad energy, aggressiveness, im-patience are what creates the famous Ego in us. We can, therefore, easily understand that when we experience Ego-centric energy, the Universe cuts itself off from us because we are here to create with God and not with the Ego, which is the opposite of Divine energy.

The "Law of Compensation" is the Law we refer to in this chapter. Compensation or redemption? That's a new question... According to the book *The Game of Life,* «Man's highest demand is for the Divine Design of his life. » When we focus *All* our energy on our life mission, we receive a lot from the Universe. Coincidences, signs, day signs, night signs (dreams), calls, intuition, luck... which is not really luck, we receive a lot. Everything goes well. Everything runs like clockwork, until we stop asking for God's help. As soon as we believe we can succeed alone, without God our Divine part, without our inner guidance that is when everything starts to go wrong. In metaphysics, it is imperative to be learning every second of our existence, to live in total union with God. When we forget our Divine part, the Ego tries to take control and that is exactly what should not happen. Man alone cannot succeed. He was made to work and collaborate in harmony with God the Creator of *All*. The healer or healing channel that thinks the energy comes from him instead of "through him" attracts many problems; the Source of many dis-eases and illnesses. Our body is a medium for communication and that is *All*. The power cord is not electricity it is a medium through which electricity passes. We receive information that we have the privilege to transmit and the mission is accomplished. This avoids many possible problems.

The sacrifice is minimal compared to what awaits us when we are truly working with the gifts God gave us. Not using them is the equivalent to not wanting to recognize what God has given us. And not being able to receive generates, over time, blockages at the level of abundance and prosperity. Hence the lack of money, health problems, stomach problems (Thomas = scepticism... stomach = estomac in French... es-Thomas), and kidney problems (liquids relating to money... in French we say liquide and in English liquid when talking about money)... In addition, remember that the game of life is to give and to receive. I spent several years, like everyone else, living with the fact that I was supporting mySelf to suit my own needs. And I was able to do it alone. I had the utmost confidence in mySelf: me, mySelf and I. When I was younger, I had faith, but when I got to "CEGEP" I took some courses in philosophy and then I studied philosophers who were against religious writings. So, I stopped asking mySelf questions about religion and God. Overwork caused me pain in the adrenal gland; the gland that secretes adrenaline. During that period, I was producing adrenaline and using it almost instantly. Overwork is *connected* to the root chakra, which is red coloured and found at the base of the spine. It is associated with survival, material needs, home, Self-confidence... I was working 70-80 hours per week at that time and I was also studying at University. I did this for several years. I had just separated and I had to buy everything: a new house, furniture, everything. I left with my old mattress and my clothes that's *All*, so... to work. We start over or at zero. Transformation. Evolution.

-._.- *-._.-* *-._.-* *-._.-* *-._.-* *-._.-*

Financial security: Security, a home and basic needs are what affect the root chakra. *All* this work was involved to acquire material goods. I had left comfort behind and now I wanted to re-find it. Yes, but at what cost? *All* this makes me dizzy. In recent years, I have been practicing the "Universal Laws" on a daily basis and I am carrying out my life mission, *All* based on what I receive as guidelines. These are directives from my intuition, Christ within me, my Divine part and my higher Self. I try to apply what I receive to the best of my ability and I am confident that I will be rewarded for my work. This is not without effort, however. I had many doubts and still do sometimes. On the other hand, now I know because more and more, I see, hear, feel, perceive, and understand. A thousand thanks to the many colours of Life!

Personal Applications

In this chapter, we are looking at the kind of person who sacrifices a lot; someone experiencing voluntary or in-voluntary sacrifice. Often, when we are passionate about an idea, we spend a lot of energy on it and consequently experience voluntary sacrifice. On the other hand, some people have to experience in-voluntary sacrifice. A person living negatively may be rather confused. She is frequently dizzy. This person could be highly obstinate, even stubborn. She will be tempted to pass judgment. She lacks a lot of discipline. Ignorance also plays a part in her life... if and of course only if, there are emotional blockages. Otherwise, a person vibrating positively will experience inspiration and it will come to her suddenly as an idea. What she knows is true *knowledge*. She has a very strong will. She lives in spiritual clarity, because she is very disciplined. Her mind is clear. She knows. She wants. She agrees with God's will. In other words, this kind of person changes from being a cynical, cold and ignorant analyst to a Master with a strong will!

To determine if there is an emotional blockage in your personal life, I suggest you take the time to answer the following questions honestly:

✓ **Are you frequently perplexed?**

If so when are you perplexed?

Have you ever felt *determined*?

What is the origin of this *determination*?

Could you re-connect to it?

Re-connect to the Source of your *determination* and imagine a Lighted rope extending from you and going to the Source of your *determination*. Ask, out loud, that you be re-connected to the Source and mentally follow the lead of the dazzling Light extending from your forehead, for example, and going to the Source. See what there is to see... feel what there is to feel... hear what there is to hear... see the colours... feel the emotions... hear the sounds and visualize the energy from that Source coming to you through this beautiful, bright cord. Experience *All* the wonderful energy filled with *determination* coming into your body... yes, that's it... feel the warmth, softness and benevolence contained in this beautiful energy. Stay united with the Source for a while... until you know you are filled with *determination*... You can return as often as you need, now that you know the way!

✓ **Are you often dizzy?**

If yes, what makes you dizzy?

Perhaps you think too much?

Do you have a lot to do?

Is your time "over-loaded"?

Are you doing what you really want to do?

Are you the type of person who works a lot to acquire material things?

If so, then it's no wonder you feel so dizzy, because you spend too much energy on non-spiritual values. In other words, you are not balanced. Your body is telling you to re-establish balance in your life. The dizziness is a sign that you are lacking something...

I suggest that, right here and now, you return to the few minutes just before the very first time you experienced dizziness. What do you notice? What is happening? Try to understand or ask yourSelf why you are going to be dizzy in a moment... What are you thinking? What are you doing? What are your emotions? Who else is there? What are you going to do? In short, write down everything you experience before becoming dizzy... then repeat the same steps for two other experiences of dizziness... Compare the three experiences... Are you experiencing the same things before becoming dizzy? What are the similarities? The similarities will provide you with a link. Take the time to analyze your experiences and you will know what to look for next time you feel your "symptoms of dizziness" coming on!

✓ **Are you a stubborn person?**

If so, when are you stubborn?

Have you ever experienced *flexibility*?

If so, why are you *flexible* at times and stubborn at others?

How could you be more *flexible*, right here and now?

I think our beliefs, values and opinions are part of our own identity, however we should not be too attached to them! Today is one thing and tomorrow will be another. Openness and *flexibility* allow for evolution since they give rise to transformation. How can you change if you are so obstinate? Besides, if you intend to evolve spiritually, you must first learn to detach yourSelf, and detachment begins with our own beliefs, ideas, points of view and values; the rest will follow. In any event, what is good for you is not necessarily good for another. We are *All* different and we *All* have different things to learn, so... again, there are a thousand and one ways to get to the same place! Do you still believe your truth is absolute?

✓ Do you tend to be judgmental?

What do you really know?

What is the purpose of making judgments?

What is hidden behind this action?

What is the Source of this action?

In the book *Twelve Steps of Forgiveness* and *A Course In Miracles*, it is shown that behind *All* actions not centered on *Love*, lies a profound lack of *Love*...

Look at when you have made judgments in the past and verify if you were somewhere, somehow missing *Love*... we forget that God is also present in our brothers and sisters... they, too, are guided as you are...

Often, people who judge are people who have been judged or mis-judged in the past and then they judge in return. Subsequently, because they judge, so others judge them. Can you see what is happening here? It's a vicious circle and the only way to stop it is to STOP JUDGING!

✓ Are you inspired by ideas that come all-of-a-sudden?

If so, then your upper forehead chakra, located midway between the third eye chakra and the crown chakra, is "harmonized". You have *Clear Thinking or Claircognizance*. You receive necessary information through sudden inspiration, sometimes without even knowing why. Or you ask a question and, soon after, you receive the answer. This is a rare gift. Note that I use the word gift here, when in reality it is not supposed to be rare... because in the beginning we *All* have the ability to possess

Claircognizance and much, much more! We can *All* have access to Universal information, but to do so we must roll up our sleeves and work a little bit: develop our skills, heal, align our chakras, do some physical exercises to be more flexible, eat well, meditate, pray and focus on Love. These are *All* things to do. That is why some authors prefer talking about gifts. Do you know a lot of people who receive information this way and who are disciplined enough to be a channel? The psychic ability that is the most widespread is empathy, Clairsentience or Clear Feeling (kinaesthetic), followed by Clairvoyance or Clear Seeing (visual), Clairaudience or Clear Hearing (auditory) and finally Claircognizance or Clear Thinking (inspiration). With time and practice, you could end up using *All* these modes of extra-sensory communication; simply send out your intention to the Universe!

N.B   Those who have the ability to receive information via Claircognizance, have an incredible opportunity because it leads to the greatest wealth and abundance of *All*! Imagine getting the information you want without even having to think about it at *All*! A real example of "Ask and you shall receive".

Chapter 13

TREASURE

.ˌ❥‿❥ˌ.

Dying the old way, forgetting the past, detachment... Detaching ourselves from values, beliefs, behaviours, ways of being, this is what the 13th tarot Arcanum is *All* about. Being able to detach ourselves is how the "Law of Transformations" works. Up to now we have discussed the small mysteries in tarot, now we are going to talk about the great mysteries; the great treasures, which follow the transformation stage, of course...

This Arcanum is related to the first astrological house, just like our friend The Juggler, which reinforces the idea that we must detach... change... transform... our personality, our "Self". That is where the treasure is hidden. Something in our lives interferes with our own evolution, something goes wrong, then we must proceed to a transformation, if not... we die the old way only to come to life again. With death there is also beginning. This is the link to our friend The Juggler; he represents new beginnings or Spring. Everything we experience is made up of death and birth. Every second, every minute, every hour, every day... death, birth, death, birth... Life!

The butterfly is an excellent symbol to illustrate transformation. Before becoming so pretty, the butterfly had to go through several transformations, so it has numerous deaths and births on its path... I am becoming more and more of a medium. Even in my dreams, which are prophetic dreams, I learn about my future. Dreams are a form of clairvoyance. I dream of what will happen in the future; the near future, distant future, but back to the present moment.

I heal. This time the healing is done with planets... three of them. I am in bed and I see them above me. Mars is above my right shoulder, Mercury above my head and Venus above my left shoulder. Healing is actually a transformation; a positive transformation. The different planets we see in dreams invite us to expand our gifts. They bring abundance and can show us some aspects of ourselves that need improving or they may encourage us to reach a balance in certain parts of our lives. Venus is above my left shoulder. It emanates Love and is the planet related to Love. Mars is above my right shoulder and brings courage and realization. Mars is the planet of action. Mercury is above my head which is the right place because it is related to communication, writing, *know*ledge and teaching. Is it a coincidence that my astrological sign is Taurus, my ascendant is also Taurus and my life companion's sign is Aries? This gives us Venus (Taurus, Libra), Mars (Aries, Scorpio) and Mercury (Cancer, Taurus). The stars are also very important in our lives. We have a star that bears our name in the Sky. After this dream, I was inspired to sleep with three different stones. The name Chantal means rock therefore crystallized information. I intuitively chose three stones that correspond to the planets seen in my dream. A pink quartz, an hematite and a black obsidian. However, I was guided about where to place them. Was this healing or transformation? Expand your gifts, have more abundance in your life, improve different facets of your life or achieve more balance. Transformation is letting the past die away... positive transformation. Inner treasures!

I am travelling, just like you, on the great journey of life; the game of life. It is the largest lottery we could win and much, much more. Life is the greatest school ever; where errors are not forgiven. When we do not understand, we repeat our mistakes again and again until we do understand. I am going to Florida to meet people I know or to meet new people. It is night time between Monday the 2nd and Tuesday the 3rd of March, 2009, which is my mother's birthday. Happy birthday dear mommy! I dreamed I was going to Florida to take a course. There were a lot of students. This dream is similar to the one I had the night of my late grandmother's birthday, April 19th 2009. My grandmother sent me messages informing me that I would participate in a course on a cruise departing from Florida. At that time I had no idea I would be going on a trip or that such a course even existed. The butterfly is a symbol of transformation and also a sign that our dearest, deceased Loved ones are with us. At least that is what Lisa Williams taught us during our course in the Caribbean in the fall of 2009. I do not often dream of my grandmother, but when I do it is a sign of great transformation in my own life. I see her, feel her and hear her... She chose birthdays to inform me that I was going to be transformed; that my life would be more feminized!

The year 2009 was a year of great changes in our home. First, just a few days after coming home from vacation, my life partner contracted an infection. This was a small occupant that did not even pay rent, but greatly damaged his environment; a tenant with no respect at *All* for other people's property. It caused a lot of damage; seven months off work for Michel and a skin graft later on. On the other hand, the ultimate goal: transformation. I also took some time off work; as the speaker, David Bernard says: «Ralentir pour mieux réussir» (Slow down for greater success). And it works pretty well, trust me! I had to and I really wanted to completely stop my activities for a while because Michel needed some help. This period allowed me to expand my gifts to another level. It was as if the Universe was rewarding me for taking care of Michel. As if the Universe was thanking me for listening. As if... simply! In addition, Michel was sitting there nearby, because he could not move very much for a few weeks, so I took advantage of the situation. I shared *All* my discoveries with him… Cool!

« *Quand les astrophysiciens découvrent une nouvelle étoile, cela ne signifie pas qu'elle est apparue à ce moment précis dans l'univers, mais seulement dans la conscience de quelques hommes. Ce qu'ils ont découvert est moins une nouvelle étoile que leur propre capacité à découvrir.* » CQPNL (extracted from the manual of practitioner in NLP).

Translation: When astronomers discover a new star that does not mean it appeared at that time in the universe, but only in the minds of some men. What they discovered is less a new star than their own ability to discover.

In *All* my being I felt that what was happening was a positive transformation for Michel and also for me. During this period, I dreamed that my late grandfather went to the hospital with Michel. He gave me a break, so I could do some personal things, like studying *A Course In Miracles* and resting. My late grandfather was watching over me. Meanwhile, Jesus was on his knees in front of me and was giving me a foot massage. Feet share a symbol with keys. Keys open doors… feet are used, among others, to achieve and manifest various desires of the Soul. This illustrates perfectly the fact that what we experience is done with the help of our Guides, allowing us to experience change, evolution, development and transformation. Sometime later, Jesus was beside Michel. I saw him and felt him. He showed me an etheric cord coming out of Michel's heart chakra; A cord which a woman later cleaned (cut) during a harmonization séance when she also noted, without anyone having mentioned it, the presence of Jesus beside Michel. Cleaning, healing, transformation brings us to buried treasures in our hearts!

♠ ♥ ♦ ♣

Personal Applications

In this chapter, we are talking about the type of person who experiences transformations in her life. She must make space to re-new. Re-new her way of thinking at the level of her beliefs; a transformation of her being, her inner being. She must experience detachment... detachments beneficial to her life mission. Yes, and one thing is certain, this will enable her to accomplish more and more. We can see an evolving being. On the other hand, a person vibrating rather negative energy will be im-patient, not grounded, removed from reality. She flits because she is very uprooted. Her breathing is very shallow which is normal: she does not experience deeply. She is too detached from the Earth. She has no perseverance... This of course, is only the case if there is emotional blockage. Otherwise, a person vibrating positive energy will be extremely patient, grounded and in touch with Earth forces. She will be very centered, since she is very anchored to the Earth. She has the power to build. She is right on Target, thanks to good sense and consistency. She goes forward with perseverance, one step after the other, one step at a time. She acts. She is anchored. She grounds herSelf. But *All* this if, and only if, she decides to actually be embodied and participate!

To determine if there is an emotional blockage in your personal life, I suggest you take the time to answer the following questions honestly:

✓ **Do you tend to be im-*patient*?**

   If so, are you lacking sleep?

   Is there something missing in your life?

   When do you tend to be im-*patient*?

Are you tolerant sometimes?

When are you more *tolerant*?

Where do you feel im-*patience* in your body? Remember a moment of im-*patience* you experienced and feel it in your own body. Where is it in your body? Do you see a colour? What colour is it? Is there anything you can associate with it? Do you hear anything? Now, where do you feel *tolerance* in your body? Remember an experience of *tolerance*... one of your most beautiful moments of *tolerance* and feel it in your body... where is *tolerance* located in you? Do you see a colour? What colour is *tolerance* in you? Is there something else you can associate it with? Hear what there is to hear? Now, imagine a possible experience when you might feel im-*patient* in the future... imagine you are experiencing it right here and now... Do you see a colour? Is it the same colour? Change the colour for the colour of *tolerance*. How does that change the experience? Repeat the exercise with two other possible experiences of im-*patience* that you might have in the future... From now on, because you have identified the colour of *tolerance*, this colour will allow you to dissolve *All* forms of im-*patience*! I suggest you work in concert with the numerous colours of life. They are the treasures of life!

✓ **Do you feel you are not grounded?**

Do you often have cold feet?

Do you ever experience a fluttering feeling?

Perhaps you are someone who does not live entirely in his physical body. You are like a fairy... or perhaps rather like an incarnate Angel. You probably have a lot of difficulty incarnating yourSelf, but you must be really grounded in order to carry out your life mission. Moreover, once

grounded, you will have some beautiful experiences...
Mother Earth gives us Love, energy, security, protection,
just like a mother. You are currently on Earth to learn, so
you must do everything to re-*connect* yourSelf to it,
otherwise what was the incarnation for? Start by taking
root. See the exercise at the end of chapter one so you will
be able to ground yourSelf properly!

✓ Is your breathing shallow?

I would suggest you do breathing exercises every day.
Breathe deeply into your abdomen. Watch your stomach
swell as you breathe. This is really relaxing because you
take time to feel each breath. Do this for twenty-one days in
a row and then it should become a habit. You will breathe
more deeply without even thinking about it. The important
thing is to live the moment fully while you are practicing
and to relax. Incidentally, this is a way to stop your little
hamster spinning!

✓ Are there times when you do not persevere?

If so, when do you not *persevere*?

Are there times when you are more consistent?

Why is it different now?

I suggest you create an affirmation. It must be <u>positive</u>. It
must be written in the <u>present tense</u>. It must be <u>precise</u>.
And you have to recite it as often as possible during the day
for three weeks.

For example:

"I am very *persistent*!"

"I am a constant person!"

"I am *persistent*, constant, constructive and I have both feet on the ground!"

"I am going forward in life with *perseverance*, step by step!"

I suggest you write your affirmation and put it in a place you will see every morning: on your bathroom mirror, your computer screen, in the kitchen or on the ceiling of your bedroom above your bed... You can also place it on your bedside table, this way you will benefit from several gifts while you sleep. Decide for yourSelf what is good for you, trust your instincts, they are always right anyway!

✓ **Do you feel you have to *detach* yourSelf from something? Something that is not good for your evolution?**

Think about the question of *detachment*. Close your eyes and let your mind guide you to your attachments... observe the links that *connect* you... Take an overview of those links. Are they bright or dark coloured? Is the energy that emanates from them Luminous or dark? Do you feel good about those links? Decide if you want to know the Source of these links and then do what you have to do to cut them if you feel the need. *Connect* yourSelf mentally to each one and feel the transfer of energy. Are they beneficial to you? Do they drain your energy? When you are *aware* of them, do you feel full or empty? If you feel drained, proceed to an energy cleansing... Observe the links that are not beneficial being cut one by one. You will feel Lightness and if a link was *connected* to a person do not be surprised if that person calls you to say that she was thinking about you today! I suggest you do the cleaning as often as you feel you have to, because we meet people every day and unfortunately, there really are vampires on Earth! By vampires, I mean people who take your energy, metaphorically, if I may say so. So that is why it is so important to cut cords, even some attachments! The more you do inner transformations the more opportunity you have to see your own "Inner Jewel"... so on your marks... Get set! Go!

Chapter 14

NEUTRALITY

◆

The ultimate goal of the preceding Arcanum (Death) was the death of the Ego. After witnessing the death of the Ego, we move from the "Law of Transformations" to the "Law of Transformation by the purification of what is obscure in the Un-*conscious*", because the aim here is to gain harmony between the psychic and material worlds; inner and outer harmony.

The Arcanum Temperance is the card of choice for professionals such as therapists, psychologists, healers, doctors, teachers, spiritual teachers, mediators, channels, mediums... The energy of this card is neutral, serene and calm. It is associated with the colour purple; the colour resulting from the perfect union between blue and red. Therefore, it is the perfect balance between passive and active. It is the perfect marriage between the feminine and masculine parts; the union of water and fire, Life and death. The creation of the Self and inner alchemy are images that emerge as well, hence the purple flame, whose creator is none other than Saint-Germain. He is one of the greatest spiritual Masters and is always working this way in Spirit...

Androgynous is the character on the card... When I studied this Arcanum, I dreamed I was a lesbian and Michel, my companion, also dreamed he was gay. Another happy coincidence! Dreaming that we make Love to someone who is the same sex as us explains that we are able to transcend an internal duality; something we could not resolve before and then finally are able to find harmony between opposites… I thank *All* the possible forms of transformation that life brings!

The energy here is the kind of energy that finally decides to let go, no longer resists and receives whatever is planned in the Universe. By letting go and receiving answers and solutions, Temperance vibrates neutrality. Yes, through neutrality and channelling, we finally receive and it could simply be answers to questions we had, and much, much more!

Without Ego, we become perfect channels between Heaven and Earth. Human rainbows… human crystals… human beings in perfect harmony… I am at an unknown location. A wise old man with long white hair is preparing potions… potions the colours of the rainbow. I know that with these potions I will heal completely. Ten months following this dream, I go to Key West and I see the old man of my dream. He does palm readings. He does a reading for me and I leave with three recipes. One was to detoxify my liver, one to improve the functioning of Michel's prostate and another for stomach problems. But, neither Michel nor I had stomach problems at that time. What a coincidence! I need it now. My stomach is not very painful, but I know the problem is because I am afraid of not having the inspiration necessary to write until the book is completely done. Our brain does not understand the difference between what is real and imagined. It does not understand the difference between different types of nourishment either: physical (food), intellectual, spiritual and emotional. I created a fear, a fear of something missing. I needed to re-focus and have faith in God as my Source. I am under Divine inspiration and I will receive the necessary nourishment. I have to fill the emptiness. My stomach (es-thomas) is reacting to my fears.

Neutrality is a characteristic that *All* good therapists, psychologists, to name a few, should have. Any healers, traditional or non-traditional, that have not healed the negative side of their Ego, cannot do healing work... Remember, we cannot give what we do not possess. An unhealed psychotherapist, for example, still believes that the attack is real, according to the writings of *A Course In Miracles*. I know a woman who was told by psychotherapists that her husband was the cause of her problems; they believed that the attack was real. It is an easy solution. Nowadays, a lot of couples separate because one of them believes the other is the Source of their problems. Nonsense! Go on vacation, you are tired and you blame the world. Take a few seconds and start looking at your own navel. Make a change in your own beliefs and you will see the situation differently. What you see is just what you see and it does not necessarily correspond to reality. In NLP we say that "the map is not the territory". The famous mirror effect... the world is a re-flection of what we are. So tell me, how do you find the world?

A good starting point for proceeding with an inner transformation is to make a list of your beliefs. Because your beliefs define you, if they are limiting, your life will also be limited and may be faulty. Your beliefs are at the center (he-*art*) of your being... Take the opportunity to improve, modify and re-move some of them from your life. Do not be surprised if you do not have a dime and you believe, for example, that the rich are thieves or that you have to work hard to succeed or that money is dirty or... any other very limiting beliefs like these.

I am asleep and then, suddenly *awake*. It is 5:30 in the morning. I have just heard a voice telling me: "My baby is about to be born, come see, Chantal!" Dream or reality? Here I have Clairaudience (Clear Hearing) or am a medium for animals! Perhaps both, there are no limits! I get up and check the bottom of my bird's cage, but there is no little bird, the egg is whole. Before I fell asleep that night, I actually heard my heart beating but it was creating a melody through the beats. I fell asleep in a state of well-being, joy and Love, as I had never experienced before. Birth symbolizes, among others, inner birth; the inner Christ. Mary gave birth to Jesus; midwife of the Soul - Soul *Awakener*, music, Celestial melody, harmony that gives birth... Birds are Heavenly messengers. They are my friends. They favour the flight of the Spirit. Christ is one of the finest examples of mediator between God and men. Am I becoming a mediator between God and my brothers and sisters on Earth? In the end, I really hope so! But let's leave it *All* to God our Father!

Personal Applications

This chapter is also about transformation; transforming what is harmful into something neutral; neutrality of our being, temperament and energy. Our role in society asks us to change so we can receive better... receive messages that are sent to us to fulfill our life mission. Our present mission can also be anything... in relation to others. Someone vibrating rather negative energy will be rigid and in-flexible. She will play the role of the opportunist. She will completely lack motivation and guidance. Her goal is twisted... if, and of course only if, there are emotional blockages. Otherwise, a person vibrating positive energy will be much more flexible and have a strong sense of adaptability. Highly mobile, she swims with the current. She is very open. She is an extraordinary Source of motivation and guidance. She accompanies. She adapts. She is the symbol of excellence and flexibility. The kind of flexibility that allows us our beautiful relationship with ourselves and with others! Go with the flow! Rowing in the same direction as the current! These are beautiful images of Temperance.

To determine if there's an emotional blockage in your personal life, I suggest you take the time to answer the following questions honestly:

✓ **Do you consider yourSelf rigid?**

  If so, when are you rigid?

  Are there times that you are more *flexible*?

  If so, when are you more *flexible*?

  The word rigid comes from the Latin word "rigidus" which means stiff? So why are you stiff?

Being rigid or stiff, means you are probably tense, which may also give rise to physical dis-ease...

To bring a little more *flexibility* into your life, I would first suggest that you do some stretching exercises so you become more *flexible* physically, which is necessary for a healthy life. Then, the image of *flexibility* in your body will make room for more *flexibility* in your relationships. Imagine you are a tree, well rooted to the ground, but moving with the flow of the wind and never being uprooted.

> *"Always fall in with what you're asked to accept.*
> *Fall in with it and turn it your way."*
>
> Robert Frost

I often use this thought because I always think I could know more. I bend to all requests, since I know that this allows me to gain *know*ledge. So I often do what others do not want to do. I must say that I am by nature very curious and I Love diversity. I have even learned to do my own oil changes. I do not do it mySelf anymore, but I know how. Knowing how...that is the goal!

✓ **Do you know what *direction* you are taking?**

Do you know where you are going?

If you don't know, when do you think you started losing *direction*?

I honestly think that your *direction* is within you in the form of your intuition. It is crying out to you, but you are not listening. Your intuition knows your *direction*, but you must be flexible and not rigid. You must allow your inner Guide to direct you without succumbing to your mind, or the conspiracy of your Ego which will try to divert your attention, and thus your *direction*. I suggest trying an exercise to learn how to listen to your intuition.

Take a few minutes to internalize... ask aloud about an issue dear to your heart. Wait a few minutes and you will receive an answer to your question mostly through your imagination. Do not block your imagination as it is a form of clairvoyance; let it be. You may not receive an answer immediately but you may receive a clue in a song or a symbol, a colour... or any other possible form. The goal is then to uncover the symbol behind what you have received. What does this song mean to you? What does that symbol mean to you? What does that colour mean to you? To understand the answer more clearly, ask again and listen... you will inevitably receive an answer. The purpose is to practice asking for directions and to be flexible enough and not resistant to possible answers; answers that may seem irrational to you, which is not important because intuition is the opposite of reason. With practice, you will work in total harmony with your inner Guide and not have any further problems with *direction*!

N.B: I suggest you keep a journal of your experiences to help you recognize your signs and the meaning of your symbols, etc.

P.-S.:   Remember: you can always make your request in writing, put it on your bedside table at night and you will receive instructions in your dreams. You can also make your request through prayer, which is another excellent way to get what you want. Praying is in fact asking!

✓ **Do you lack *motivation*?**

If so, when do you lack *motivation*?

Do you know what the Sources of your *motivation* are?

If so, what are they?

If you lack *motivation* for an activity, is it possible for you to combine this activity with a Source of *motivation* that you adore? For example, you could exercise while listening to music, cook while listening to music, walk while listening to audio books or courses or run inside on a training machine while reading. Even when you do something that demands concentration you can listen to instrumental music like new-age music, for example. Furthermore, this kind of music is relaxing. I do a lot of things while listening to music. I have always worked with it. I vary the style according to my needs. When I want to be more *connected*, I often listen to the "OM" (a spiritual sound that opens our third eye chakra and elevates the vibration). I prefer listening to music that lifts my vibratory rate when I write. It has also been proven that this kind of music gets rid of negative energy, so this way I am sure to channel Love energy. The same applies to you. How then, can you change your activities, or other things for which you lack *motivation*, by bringing a touch to them that will *motivate* you? As they say in NLP: "The small difference that makes *All* the difference!"

✓ **Do you have trouble *letting go*?**

Many of us have trouble *letting go*, and this is normal: we have followed the same programming for many years, even for many lives. On the other hand, if you want to receive an energy greater than you, regardless of your goal, you must *let go*. We have preconceived ideas, beliefs and values: this is what we are. We are made of beliefs, ideas and values. That is why we are *All* unique. However, if we do not *let go*, we are unable to receive *All* the solutions. By keeping an open mind, we create space to receive, like a child who seems lacking in *know*ledge and at the same time open to receive it *All*.

As I explained in the previous chapter, I had to apply *letting go* at the beginning of 2009. While returning from vacation with my life partner, I planned and organized my coming months. However, I had to put my projects aside for a while, because Michel was seriously ill. We spent more than forty hours in the hospital during the first week and that continued for several months. In the beginning during the first week, I was annoyed as they say. Then I calmed down and I just accepted the situation. From that moment on, *All* proceeded like clockwork. As soon as I had *let go* and opened up to new horizons, my gifts began appearing in my life. I developed my gifts much faster than I would have done normally. I was available and ready at the same time.

Another example of *letting go* in my life is when I want to carry out a task with which I am not particularly familiar or when I am too tired to perform it properly. I *let go* and am receptive about how to do it. In the past, I tended to panic or get angry because of my lack of *know*ledge or my fatigue which reduces my patience. Now, I re-focus at the heart level and I am guided to do what I am doing. Wonderful, isn't it? I am no different from you... The key is simple; remain "Neutral"!

Chapter 15

THE MATERIAL WORLD
o0×X×0o

In this chapter we will discuss our exaggerated interest in the material. Temptation is our little inner devil. On the other hand, it can also be a great creative force; the ability to make real what we need... and much, much more. In tarot, The Devil is the card related to MONEY among other things. The ultimate goal is to be able to enjoy what we possess freely but not to be possessed by it!

When the energy of this card is positive, we have the strength of a lion, instead of a sheep... but we still have to exceed our abilities and assert ourselves: assert our own personality. Ouch! In the long run, there are blockages causing impotence. There is free movement of our own strength and the freedom to express our true individuality... without cutting ourselves off from the rest of humanity!

Here, we are talking about masculine energy; Yang energy in *All* its splendour, hence its resemblance to our friend The Emperor. They are both entrepreneurs. The Emperor is very protective, but The Devil can be very Self-centered at times. His energy is the opposite of Temperance's because he feels pulled in many directions at the same time, while she is centered, poised and serene.

When you spend a lot of energy acquiring material things, it is normal that at some point, you feel pulled by several strings in many directions. Do not be surprised if you feel un-*balanced* or even dizzy. The desire to satisfy your desires, yes, but at what cost? This Arcanum corresponds to the third astrological house;

it is exactly the opposite of our friend The Empress. The Empress creates and communicates using ordered forces, while The Devil, tends towards dis-order, chaos, division or separation. However, it is *All* necessary for evolution. He is under the influence of the "Law of Diabolic Forces" and he is subject to the Universal Law of Justice.

I understand clearly that I am here to learn and help others, like you, in fact, through my experiences. Learning to learn... Opening yourSelf is a very good remedy to overcoming the evil forces represented by The Devil. New, open ways of thinking that can be detached from that which destroys or stagnates. The aim to be incarnate is to enjoy freely what life wants to give us. What it decides to give us.

I am in a pharmacy with my boyfriend. An old man is standing there and he is looking at me. I feel attracted to him, so I go over to meet him. He is tall, wears a long coat and has an extraordinary aura. He says, "you have the flu!" But I do not have the flu... flu manifests itself in our lives when we experience a "territorial conflict" (conflit de territoire) or "dispute conflict" (conflit de dispute). It means to be restrained from our own freedom; freedom of movement, thought and speech. It is as if our rights and freedoms are violated. Influenza equals influence, the evil influence of the Devil. An example would be the un-*conscious* over-protection of some mothers sometimes.

I was travelling with a friend who in the end I did not know. I felt that my rights were violated. I could not even express mySelf freely. Even the way I dressed was criticized. We were experiencing a "territorial conflict" or "dispute conflict". I came back from that trip and I caught the flu and was ill for a whole month... a month bedridden without energy. Have a companion, yes, but at what cost? We should not care what others wear. The habit does not make the monk! Everything was my fault; I did not respect mySelf, and I did not express mySelf; which is the opposite of my own personality, but I was afraid to hurt. Confined in the same energy bubble for several days, even weeks, in the end the energy infected me. Based on this experience, I would strongly advise you to be careful with whom you share your energy, because in the long run you can become very sick without knowing why. This is quite normal: the energy of others touches our own and if we are un-protected or tired, then BOOM! Here's a gift. Nevertheless, remember that this was *All* predestined! The goal, the ultimate goal is to learn!

In the book *The Game of Life,* it is written that "The only enemy of man is "fear", fear of poverty, failure, illness, loss, all feelings of insecurity at any level whatsoever". Jesus Christ said: "Why are ye fearful, oh ye of little faith?" (Matt.8:26) Unfortunately, our fears have been passed from generation to generation, like an in-*heritance*... from generation to generation or even from life to life. They are a part of our luggage that we carry with us for centuries and centuries.

I personally know many of my own fears: fear of commitment, fear of success, fear of fame... So, to help me overcome my fears, for example, I create beautiful affirmations like this: "I release mySelf, here and now, from the fears I experience... Starting today, I will go forward on my life path with joy and pleasure and release my Soul of *All* fears and be very successful." I suggest you create your own affirmation. You can even put it on your beside table and you will be able to integrate it fully during sleep. Dreams help with healing, understanding and seeing, among others. Why not take advantage of them? This tool is available to *All* and gives us answers to our numerous questions.

♠ ♥ ♦ ♣

Personal Applications

In this chapter, we are looking at the type of person who has an exaggerated interest in the material world. Someone who is too attached to everything, near or far, related to the material. This attachment can also involve people; for example, a person who forgets she is incarnate here in this body which is in fact also material and will return to dust. There is no balance. She is not free. She is struggling inside and does not realize it. She imposes herSelf. She forces things. She feels excluded and is thereby excluded. She is Self-centered. She is very grumpy. The rebel, the quarreller, the ones who always want to be right are examples of archetypes vibrating in negative energy... if and of course only if, there are emotional blockages. Otherwise, a person who vibrates in a positive way will prefer the following roles: the crew companion, competitor or fighter. This person fights for something beneficial. She will participate actively with others. She will have great ability for cooperation. She will have the ability to reach her goals. She grows through conflicts, understanding that she is learning every step of the way. She knows what her purpose is. She lives with the belief that we are *All* together, united, from life to life!

To determine if there is an emotional blockage in your personal life, I suggest you take the time to answer the following questions honestly:

✓ **Do you tend to have an exaggerated interest in the material world?**

If so, what would happen if you were to lose what you have?

How far are you willing to go to acquire things?

The purpose of our incarnation is, among others, to *enjoy* what we have, otherwise why have we chosen to incarnate?

-._.- *-._.-* *-._.-* *-._.-* *-._.-* *-._.-*

This is a great difference from the other world. However, we must control ourselves. We must control temptation. And we must savour each moment, without being dependent. The material world exists, we must *enjoy* it, but it stops there.

Do you have goods just for the sake of having them? In other words are you a collector?

In metaphysics, it is taught that abundance is for everyone without exception. However, we are also taught that when we accumulate, we are in violation. This is a violation that touches the "Law of free Movement (free Circulation)". To own thirty-six pairs of shoes, ninety-nine necklaces or a collection of thirteen cars does not, in any way, alter the Spiritual Laws. What is bad is not using them. That is an infraction! There is congestion of free movement! Material things are created to be used, not to be venerated. Veneration belongs to the Divine world.

✓ **What are you attached to?**

What is worth the price of your life mission?

You arrived alone and you will return alone. Therefore, tell me why you spend so much energy fighting against a plan that you chose before your incarnation?

«Man's highest demand is for the Divine Design of his life.»

From the book: The Game of Life.

Any other interest is secondary... The only interest to which you should give *All* your energy is God's purpose, your Divine plan. Your goal is to discover your Divine purpose and then spend *All* your energy on it! You must find the path of your Higher-Self. So... BE, and BE it now!

-._.- *-._.-* *-._.-* *-._.-* *-._.-* *-._.-*

✓ What kind of conflicts do you attract?

Do you have trouble in your relationships?

Can you remember your last conflict with another person?

If so, then pretend you are sitting in front of this person now... you can see her/him... smell her/him... hear your conversation... Remember your discussion... What is going on? What do you see exactly? How do you feel? What do you hear? Take note of what you experienced at that time precisely. Then do the same thing, but this time putting yourSelf in the shoes of the other person. To do this, I suggest you sit in another chair, the other person's chair... you can see yourSelf... you can smell yourSelf... you can hear yourSelf... Remember the discussion... What is going on in the skin of the other? What do you see through her/his eyes? What do you feel in her/his body? What do you hear through her/his ears? Take note of what you experience at that time in her/his place... How do you see yourSelf through the eyes of someone else? Do you still believe you are right? Look at the situation from another angle... Take your own place in the script... Now, how did the person, who was with you, feel? What were her/his views? Why do you think she/he did what she/he did? What were her/his positive intentions?

The way we see things differs depending on the position we take. And unfortunately, too many conflicts have their Sources in INTERPRETATION. Again, according to our numerous differences (beliefs, values, cultures, educations...), we interpret and see things differently. Ultimately, we are *All* right... ACCORDING TO WHAT WE KNOW!

✓ *Visualize the elbows and solar plexus chakras – liver,* **stomach and kidneys problems**

Elbows are joints that are *connected* in energy to the solar plexus chakra. So do not be surprised if you have a liver problem (anger, irritation) or a stomach problem (repressed feelings) or a problem in the small intestine and that you also have some issues with your elbows. The meridians of your elbows are secondary chakras that may have problems if you have a blockage or anything else at the solar plexus level...

References: *Le Livre des 28 Chakras*, Élias Wolf.

Visualize the meridians of your elbows turning clockwise in a beautiful yellow hue. And imagine the solar plexus chakra turning at the same time with the same colour. They work together in harmony. You can also visualize these chakras in a dark blue, which is in fact the complementary colour of the chakra. Visualize them yellow and blue or blue and yellow, as you wish. Emit your intention to align your chakras. Stay in that state for as long as necessary and let the work happen on its own!

✓ **Do you tend to force issues?**

If so, why do you do it?

When, exactly, do you tend to force things?

Do you think that forcing is similar to exaggerating or violating?

By replacing the word "force" with the word "violate", for example, does that make you want to improve your situation?

I would ask you to go back fifteen minutes prior to the last time you forced something in the past... now, see the situation as though you were "violating" the space, environment, rights... of others... How does that make you feel? Would you still force things or would you rather let them be?

Personally, I try never to force anything in my life. Anyway, whenever I have forced things in the past, it was not good at *All*! I believe that when we force the course of events, events that are not supposed to be, life itself puts us back on track. When I wrote this book, I experienced moments when I had to give free rein to life. Several times I wanted to write, but was not inspired. It was not the time to be productive. If I had listened to certain people around me, I would have forced the issue, but it was not a question of what "I" wanted, but what I was not meant to do at that time. I accept who I am, I am a channel, among others, and I receive what I am meant to write and say, that's *All*.

Chapter 16

HIGHER CONSCIOUSNESS

In tarot the Arcanum The Tower asks us to be open to our Higher *Consciousness*. It symbolizes en*light*enment, *light*ning, fire, destruction, loss and purification, to allow us an ELEVATION.

In the language of the Soul, which is a symbolic or metaphorical language, the house symbolizes the "Self". Thus, the house of God or the Tower represents the destruction of a part of our "Self". We are asked to change our way of thinking, acting or communicating. We are strongly advised to change one of our values, beliefs, in short a part of ourSelf that identifies us.

Some people do not want to see the changes suggested by life. They act as though they do not understand, like an ostrich with its head in the sand. Then one day, a test is imposed; sickness, separation, bankruptcy, any kind of loss. This is what that card has to offer. It attracts the "Law of the Balance of Opposites".

I am asleep and I know I am in a near death state. My physical body is still lying on the bed. However, my Soul is elsewhere... in another world... in the in-*visible* world. A world where God is. A world in which I seek teaching and healing and much, much more! I feel the presence of God. I do not see him, but I know he is there. I smell his spicy aroma, as if he smelled like ginger for example. Roots. Our roots. When we dream at night, this is what happens. Our body is lying and our Soul flies to re-Source itself. This explains why, among others, we experience impressions of "déjà vu". Of course, through meditation, hypnosis or other forms of concentration like relaxation, we can experience altered states of *consciousness*. That is why, for example, it is so good to practice meditation at least 15-20 minutes per day. According to some, those 15-20 minutes of meditation are equivalent to an hour of sleep.

The Tower (God's house) pictured on this Arcanum is not built on a solid foundation. Therefore, we have to destroy so we can re-build on a new base. When we live a life of falsehoods, it can not last indefinitely. We must broaden our horizons to achieve greater "clear vision". A clearer picture of our lives.

After the fire, greenery starts to grow again and becomes stronger than ever. Water, wind and fire purify. They clean everything in their path. But they seem to destroy what has been built; built in-correctly.

Here we can see the *fall*; *fall* of the king. The King who believes he knows everything and who has, according to him, the absolute truth. The truth for *All*. We are witnessing the inevitable death of the monarchy. God's house (The Tower) is the sixteenth Arcanum in tarot and is also associated with the fourth astrological house. This Arcanum has the energy of an emperor whose accomplishments are not compatible with those of God's plan, our Divine Plan. Sometimes when our achievements are not compatible with those of God's, what happens has to happen... Life stops what we were doing or puts us in another direction. We always have the choice, but is it the right choice? That's why we're talking about the balance of opposites.

I am on vacation with Michel, my spiritual companion. We are by the sea. The sea is the best place for me to re-Source mySelf. I feel at home. We are moving towards a beautiful house and, suddenly, I realize it is mine or rather ours. We bought a house on the seashore Wow! I am blessed. It is located on a mountain. We can see the sunrise and sunset every day. I had this dream when I was studying The Tower Arcanum. It reinforces the fact that there are changes that must inevitably occur in our lives. Changes that touch our "Self". Purchases reveal the state of our health, our energy, our business. The greater our buying powers, the better our health, because health and business go hand in hand... Then if you are able to buy yourSelf a new house in your dreams, this foretells a wedding, your own wedding. Union with an inner Divinity. Union with *All* the parts of yourSelf complete. In my case, marriage with Michel (Michael)... If the trend continues, normally within six to eighteen months following the dream, the reality happens. I will get married and buy a new house. A house by the sea. Hawaii is a fantastic place, full of beautiful and good energy, but I will leave that to God for he guides me on my Divine Path.

Our values, our beliefs are our "Self" and often they come from our roots... These roots so deeply rooted... Addiction problems, bitterness, just to name a few, can also be part of our roots and they may be behaviours you have copied. Have you thought of that? Are they really your emotions? You were raised with people who vibrate at a particular frequency and you were in their energy field. So, what do you think now? Forgiveness is the solution. Forgive yourSelf first and then forgive what happened. This is part of your life experience. Everything happens for a reason. This is when your heart chakra will un-lock, allowing Love to flow freely. As it should be. Green. Healing or ressurrection?

At first glance, The Tower reveals to us a sense of loss or a period of questioning; chaos. And from chaos will flow joy! Personally, I believe it is necessary to question ourselves from time to time. It allows us to see more clearly. We can hear better. It enables us to feel more and more. Since we have probably failed to witness the death of the Ego, we must now stop it completely.

Your body is the temple you inherited to receive your inner God. To do this, you must purify yourSelf. Do not wait to be struck by *lightning*! That is the advice of a friend. A friend for life!

Personal Applications

This chapter is about the person whose foundations are collapsing. This person has lived for a long time with bases that are more or less solid and life has tested her to improve her destiny. Tests and initiations are part of evolution; the evolution of a man or woman who has beliefs and values that are damaging to their life path. Anyone vibrating in a vortex of negative energy will tend to steal it *All*. She grabs everything for herSelf. She keeps it *All* and shares nothing. She pushes everything away on her path, instead of bringing things together. She leads. She is the mastermind. Her purpose is to succeed, un-*consciously*, by getting rid of everything... if and of course only if, there are emotional blockages. Otherwise, a person vibrating positive energy will know how to balance giving and taking in equal amount. She takes and she gives. She gives and she receives. She has a sense of sharing. Sharing is a part of her life. She no longer resists the multiple signs of life. She recognizes. She listens. She follows her intuition more and more!

To determine if there is an emotional blockage in your personal life, I suggest you take the time to answer the following questions honestly:

✓ **Have you undergone or are you currently undergoing one of life's tests?**

If so, do you understand why?

If not, take note of the test...

Is it an illness?

What kind of illness is it?

Your body is talking to you through that precise illness. What is it trying to tell you? Ask it, it will answer you. In your mind, go and meet the part of you that is trying to tell you something. Talk to it as if it was a person. The illness is a form of energy and because everything is energy, it is also a form of life... Ask it what it wants to tell you... then, when you understand the message, thank it. Thank the part of you that sent you a message for your evolution; your healing. And ask the illness, kindly, to return to its Source... see it returning to its Source surrounded by a bright, white Light.

Is it bankruptcy or a loss?

What do you think you have you lost?

Did it really belong to you?

Have you ever failed to pay someone for something ?

Have you ever done something dis-honest in your life?

Whatever the reason, one thing is certain, an energy re-balancing is now necessary in your life. You must open yourSelf to your Higher *Consciousness*. Right now there is too much negative energy in your life and you have to re-focus on the energy of Love, Light and Truth and you cannot get there alone. You must join an energy Higher than yours. You just have to express your desire to open yourSelf to your Higher *Consciousness* while having faith, feeling it in every cell of your body, and before long, you will feel *connected*... You will feel bigger or larger in energy only; as if you were inflated. Inflated as in full. You will be filled with Light. You will be a channel... A channel of Light. But to succeed, you must first open yourSelf up! Open the door of your he-*art*!

✓ **Are you the kind of person who takes everything in your path?**

If so, what exactly do you help yourSelf to?

Why do you steal things?

What is the purpose of stealing it *All*?

Personally, I know people who have this awful habit. They put their hands on everything and anything. Unfortunately, they also have many health issues. They do not see anything that life, in vain, tries to show them. This reminds me of a movie. A man rings the doorbell of a house inhabited by a couple and their only son. The man tells the couple that if they press the button on a box he has with him they will receive a million dollars. The consequence of this act is that a person they do not know will die. They have twenty-four hours to think about it. The couple has financial problems at that time. They talk it over, but the husband does not agree. Finally, the wife presses the button and they receive the million dollars as promised, but a misfortune also occurs: their only son contracts a fatal dis-*ease* and the only way he will get better is if the husband kills his wife. That way, the wife's Soul will heal and the son will also be healed, which is exactly what ends up happening. This film conveys several important messages. We can also see why it is so important for each of us to heal our various wounds. Whenever one of us heals, we *All* heal! So I beg you, heal yourSelf! If you do not want to do it for yourSelf, do it for your children! They are your inheritors...

✓ *Beliefs* **list – limiting beliefs**

I suggest that you write a list of *All* your *beliefs*. Write everything that you believe, and afterwards verify the ones that are limiting and those that are not. A limiting *belief* is a *belief* that limits your life. For example, having to work hard to succeed is a limiting *belief*, since it implies that you always need to work hard if you want to succeed, otherwise you will not succeed. This is not ALWAYS the case and we are lucky it is not!

BELIEFS	LIMITING	NON LIMITING
I have to work hard to succeed.	χ	
I can do anything!		χ
Money is dirty.	χ	
My intuition guides me.		χ
If I do not exercise every day, I will gain weight.	χ	
What ever happens, it's always right.		χ

✓ **Homework: compliment yourSelf as much as possible... and help others...**

Now I will ask you to compliment yourSelf as often as possible during the next week or so. Help an elderly person to cross the street or give someone something to eat or feed an abandoned animal... Give as much as you can during the next week and then notice what comes back to you... When you receive things, accept everything, no matter what. Your reward from God is in the hands of whomever He decides. Do not judge. If the person giving seems poorer than you, do not judge, this comes from God. Remember, it is not good to make judgments like that. Keep a journal of your experiences, so you can see how life rewards you. The goal here is to play the game of life, which is "give and you shall receive"!

✓ The hand meridians are *connected* to the heart chakra...

Your hand meridians are *connected* to those of your heart. When you do not do what you really want, do nothing or do bad things, your meridians are choked and the energy is altered. We then observe the emergence of problems with the heart chakra, because the two are *connected*. Do not be surprised if someone you know has heart complications and he is dis-*interested*, has no goals, no projects... hands were created to accomplish our projects. No more projects, no more Love of life. To correct this type of blockage, I suggest you start and finish a project, regardless of the size, and do it with *All* your heart. Otherwise, do nothing at *All*. And if you are going to do something that is not beneficial, think twice before doing it. Think about your health first. Ask yourSelf this question before doing anything: "Am I in harmony with mySelf and the rest of the Universe if I do...?". When you have an idea, re-focus on your heart and feel if it agrees with you, if it does, carry out your idea with both hands. In the past (and still in some countries today), justice literally cuts off the hands of those who steal, for example. This is no longer the case but remember that beyond human Justice there is a Universal ONE, and that is the ONE you must fear! It is in-*visible* to our eyes, but very *visible* when it wants to show us our lack of integrity, our alienation from the Truth.

Chapter 17

INTUITION

A fter passing through the The Devil Arcanum which forces us to detach from the material world and then The Tower that causes breakdowns, we re-discover the calm after the storm. The Star is the card in tarot which is like a Light, a Guide, an opening in the mental barriers that we had to break down in the previous arcana. Under the same star as the High Priestess (The Female Pope), The Star opens the way to even more wealth. If we listen carefully, it shows us the way home. This information is transmitted through our own intuition.

The Star asks us to work in concert with silence where it ressembles the High Priestess. We are asked here to return to "the heart of silence"... The seventeenth Arcanum in tarot is associated with the fifth astrological house, which means creativity, sexuality, children. It reminds me of the Source of the sacral chakra which is the chakra linked to the High Priestess.

The energy that emanates from this Arcanum is entirely female. Femininity in *All* its splendor. Pure yin energy, whose aim is to work easily with intuition. Intuition is like a Star... it shows the right direction.

One night, I *woke* up to go to the bathroom. It was not something I was used to doing, but it happened. Returning to bed afterwards, I stopped at the window for a certain length of time and there was a very bright star before me. I looked at it and returned to bed un-*conscious* of what had just happened. It was only the next morning that I realized what had really happened. That evening, I wrote a dream affirmation that I put on my beside table before going to sleep. I wrote: "Tonight, I am going to meet my Guides to thank them." Now I really know that I come from the stars. Our energy is like that of the stars. That is why you can, thanks to the energy in your hands, remove *All* non-beneficial Sources contained in your food, for example, or heal yourSelf by placing your hands on the illness.

The Star is a card that gives a lot of hope. Its energy is optimistic. Because it is the first Arcanum that touches the Cosmic world, it opens the path to mystical illumination. The night begins with The Star Arcanum, then it gives place to The Moon which represents the phase of re-vival, and it leads us to The Sun Arcanum, the *awakening*...

This card is associated with creativity, children and sexuality and announces birth; mystical birth... creating a work of *art*. In dreams, babies can symbolize various projects and realizations, births and creations present in our lives.

During the study of this Arcanum, I was guided to look very closely at the importance of pets in our lives. Several signs have come into my life so I would be informed about this. I read an article on pet therapy that fell into my hands by coincidence. I received an email on therapy with horses. I even took note of my own behaviour and feelings with my cats and those of people around me with theirs. With animals, we can really experience *unconditional* Love. They are in our lives to help us eliminate negative energy. My cat was my living indicator of negative energies. I have seen him going out of the house backwards, because there was someone inside with negative energy. I sincerely believe that this cat was sent to me by God for healing and working with energy. If you pay attention, you notice, that when there is something wrong in your life, your pet's as well as your children's health are affected. Animals and children are just like sponges. They are hyper-sensitive and feel everything. The next time your cat, dog or child is sick, take time to observe what is happening in your own life...

I believe animals can also serve as physical bodies for the Spirits of deceased, Loved ones. This is another great mission they may inherit. Yes, for example, a Loved one dies and feels the need to continue taking care of you. He could then choose to come back, for a certain period, in the body of a pet. This way the Spirit can come back faster than by being reincarnated in a human body. That is why it is important to give lots of Love to any living being. They are *All* here invested in a very special mission that nobody else can do in their place, like you and me, so... who are you to judge?

Femininity is the ultimate sex in this Arcanum. This Arcanum helped me understand some blockages in my second chakra; the sacral chakra governing creativity, procreation and sexuality. In her book *Sacred Contracts,* Caroline Myss declares that we *All* possess the archetype of the prostitute. This archetype has long prevented me from using my creativity and sexuality. Women are not the only ones to have this archetype, you too gentlemen! Therefore, when you are paid for your talent, you are considered to have the prostitute archetype. In this sense, no one can escape! Ouff, thank you God, another problem solved!

While studying The Star Arcanum, I was also guided to change my diet again. For more that five years, my diet has been mainly vegetarian. I was advised, through my dreams, to adopt this diet. The goal is to eliminate more and more of the toxins and chemicals that interfere with my receptivity of heavenly messages within a time frame that suits me. The purpose is to be able to hear more clearly the messages sent to me, for mySelf and others. That night, before falling asleep, I asked God to please tell me if there was anything else I needed to do to continue my beautiful life mission. As usual, he answered me!

Throughout the study of this card, I also realized that my life mission was very closely related to books. Although I have always Loved to read, I had never thought about writing a book! Teaching yes, but not writing a book even though I have always Loved to write… In the months following, I was guided to take a course with Nathalie Hamelin: "Comment réaliser votre projet d'écriture." (How to realize your writing project.) I also started my own publishing company: "Les Éditions Chantou" and so on, until I started writing this book full-time. This Arcanum also represents the archetype of the artist; the artist who has one foot in the water (emotions, spirituality) and the other on Earth (materialization). This is creativity and inspiration under the symbol of the lion, and not that famous little sheep anymore… The strength of the lion guided by his intuition!

Personal Applications

This chapter is about the 'Soul Chakra', that is to say, the chakra where *All* our archetypes, experiences and *know*ledge reside; the place where our past lives are crystallized. Where *All* our baggage is located. Here we are talking primarily about someone who must learn to work with her intuition. She is emotional and that is what gives her her wings; an artistic Soul, creative and very feminine. She guides, because she knows her own internal Guide. She is in a period of rest so she can learn to receive everything that she needs to pursue her destiny... A person vibrating negative energy will be rather naïve. The image she projects is of absence, hence the emergence of a possible mental problem. Schizophrenia could be a possibility. Division is part of her plan... if and of course only if, there are emotional blockages. Otherwise, a person who vibrates positive energy will vibrate through the purity of her heart and innocence. She will generate great confidence and unrivaled integrity with a lot of authenticity! Instead of playing the role of profiteer or hypocrit, she will be the image of the child and at the same time of the radiant woman (man). She now listens to her Higher Self. She also listens to the voice of her Soul. She is united to everyONE. She recognizes karmic experiences. And *All* this, because she works in concert with her intuition!

To determine if there is an emotional blockage in your personal life, I suggest you take the time to answer the following questions honestly:

✓ **Do you have difficulty *receiving*?**

Do you feel un-comfortable when someone gives you something?

If so, when does this happen?

In your opinion, why is it so difficult for you to *receive*?

Can you remember an experience in which it was hard for you to *receive* what was offered? I would ask you now, please, to put yourSelf in the shoes of that person at that time... feel what she felt when you refused her gift... Now, reverse the situation and you are the person who is giving and what you want to give is refused... How do you feel? Is it any different for someone else?

Learning to *receive* is a prerequisite to working with your intuition. Not resisting what life gives us is a great quality. In addition, it opens doors to greater abundance. Resisting, stops it!

✓ *The Soul chakra...*

The Soul chakra is a supra-personal chakra located above the crown chakra, about a hand's width above the head. If you close your two hands, forming a ball above your head you will touch it, you can feel it too. Visualize it as a ball of energy the size of an orange or a grapefruit, for example. It is a steel blue colour. Touch it with the palms of your hands; you will feel a lot of heat. *Connect* to the seat of your Soul by touching it or simply by imagining it and ask it to send you a message... a message for your healing or a symbol so that you can understand something related to your past, for example... This chakra contains *All* the information about your identity for this life, as well as your past lives. How do you feel? What do you see? What do you hear? Stay in this position for as long as you like. You may see a colour, image or symbol... you may hear a sound, song or voice... you may feel an emotion, a vibration or a feeling... Let your Soul speak to you and then try to interpret the message it is sending you!

Again, I suggest you keep a journal of your experiences. You can repeat this exercise as often as you wish. The more you practice, the more you will understand the messages from your Soul. The goal here is to interpret the messages it sends you. If you have received a message in the form of a symbol, a colour, a sound, a song... what does it mean to you? Write it down and ask for more information if you need it...

✓ **Experiencing unification with your Soul...**

Now I would like to guide you through a meditation to help you experience Union with your Soul... Close your eyes... Relax your entire body... feel the well-being, peace and wholeness in every cell of your being... See, hear, feel, a flame, a spark, there just in the middle of your being... feel the benefits of this beautiful flame... feel the warmth of this beautiful spark... spark of joy, Love, Divine Light... peace... your Soul... your Divine part... right there inside you... then imagine the flame spreading peacefully to *All* parts of your body... see it, feel it, hear it going down through your body, your stomach, your hips, your legs, your feet and into your toes... then, see it, hear it, feel it going up to your neck, across your shoulders, your arms, your elbows, your hands, your fingers and, finally, into your head.. you are united with your Soul... you and your Soul are ONE... then you see an opening on the top of your head... this is the opening to the crown chakra... where we channel... the opening for channelling... then move to the Soul chakra located a hand-width above the crown chakra... you are ONE with the Soul chakra... stay there a while... what are you experiencing? Do you see anything? How do you feel?

What do you hear? This chakra is actually where the Soul returns when the physical body has completed its mission, so that is why *All* your past is stored in this exact place... it's like a stone that is engraved with *All* your personal history since the birth of your Soul... Take the opportunity to meet each other... stay there as long as you want... then return in the next minute, to the here and now, bringing with you *All* the benefits of this wonderful experience!

✓ **Do you find it difficult to listen to the voice of your intuition?**

I suggest you do an exercise to practice listening to your *intuition.*

Take a deck of cards; the goal here is to listen to your *inner voice.* Chose a regular deck of cards, with Diamonds, Spades, Clubs and Hearts. Pick a card at random, without looking. Then try to guess its suit. Is it Spades, Clubs, Diamonds or Hearts? Check. Do this until you can guess fairly regularly which suit it is and when you feel ready, proceed to the second step. Pick a card again at random without looking and this time, be more precise, saying which figure appears on the card. Is it an Ace, King, Queen, Jack, 10, 9, 8, ... ? Then check. Do this until you can guess fairly regularly which figure or number appears on the card. When you feel you are ready to move to the next level, pick a card at random and be even more precise. Name the card you have in your hands. Is it a Queen of Diamonds, King of Spades, Ace of Hearts, ... ? This type of exercise allows you to work with your *intuition.* The more you practice an exercise like this, the more you work in concert with your *inner voice,* your internal Guide.

You can also try to figure out who is calling when the phone rings. With pratice and time, you can guess who will be calling within a few seconds!

You can also practice with a friend by trying to guess what he is thinking: a colour, number, letter... However, I suggest you begin by narrowing the range of possibilities and increasing it at your own pace. For example, start with five or ten items at a time, then increase them with practice.

The trick is to empty your mind completely beforehand, so you are able to receive. Forget the competition and instead be in reception mode...

Chapter 18

THE UN-CONSCIOUS
☺

The Arcanum under discussion here is The Moon… the most karmic Arcanum in tarot and the link to the un-*conscious*. It is the eighteenth card and is found under Pisces in the Zodiac. This sign is associated with the twelfth astrological house: the family shadow, the family un-*conscious*, the un-*conscious*…

According to Jung, everything that is not in the *conscious* mind is therefore buried in the un-*conscious*. There is the personal un-*conscious*, the collective un-*conscious* and the archaic un-*conscious*… At night, when we sleep, we are in an altered state of *consciousness*, in a state other than a *conscious* one. We are, among others, in the world of the un-*conscious*. We may also experience altered states of *consciousness* during meditation, while driving a car, reading a book, under hypnosis… any activity that allows us to stop mental activity and focus. Thus we can access a parallel world, the world of the un-*conscious*. With a little practice we can be *conscious* during our dreams at night. This is called lucid dreaming. I often have lucid dreams. I am *aware* of certain facts which exist in my every day life and I can transpose them into my dreams at night. That's why I believe it is so important to understand our un-*conscious* symbols or the symbols that our sub*conscious* uses. As I have already explained, there is no difference, in my opinion, between day signs and night signs (dreams). In both cases, the language used is the language of the Soul… Symbolic language… Metaphorical language… The sub*conscious* also uses symbols, since the Soul travels in these parallel worlds…

The Moon is a feminine energy, illuminated by the reflection of Light from The Sun; the next Arcanum. On its own, it is in total darkness. The imagination is much exploited here; it is even a great strength, but only as a separate being not as being ONE with the Spirit. The only faith that is practiced here is focusing on intellectual abilities. The only possible way to know any truth is through the mind. Illusion and separation are paths too often taken. We are witnessing a period of deep sleep... REM sleep, during which we dream... but now they have discovered that we dream in other periods too... a period of extreme darkness before reaching Sunlight, if any.

The Moon and The Sun are ONE of three couples in tarot. When we integrate this last couple, we really become a complete being. We are now talking about the cosmic or mystical couple; the *conscious* and un-*conscious* as ONE; female and male becoming Divine again. It is the marriage of Heaven and Earth.

We have talked about the fact that this Arcanum is karmic. The Law of Rhythm is under its influence. Karmas are cyclical. They come back to haunt us until we become *aware*. Then there is passage from the un-*conscious* level to the *conscious* level and the healing process of this lesson takes place. According to some writings, there would be eclipses of the sun and moon. They follow a cycle of 18 years. The Moon is the 18th Arcanum in tarot. The number 18 is double; we are talking about Light and darkness, white and black, positive and negative, both sides of the coin. Nine multiplied by two equals eighteen, which makes this dear lady Moon a Hermit twice!

The energy of this Arcanum shows us we need to clarify and deepen what is cyclical or repetitive in our lives. Perhaps even deepen in meditation, for example, to understand something related to our present life and also to our previous lives. To be able to see and understand repetitive cycles and to recognize their origins, roots... THEIR SOURCES. Repetitions are un-*conscious* behaviours that are imprisoned and waiting to be released. As soon as you start trying to understand how karma works, you are at the beginning of en*light*enment. We carry with us patterns as old as our Soul. Day and night, we receive clues and signs that excite our curiosity and make us more *conscious* of the repetitive or cyclical phenomena occurring in our lives. Do you really believe that your "sickness" belongs to you?

Enjoying life with a lot of fight and great Self-confidence is a key to Self-realization. However, knowing its roots and origins, allows us to analyze and understand what is secretly hidden in the deepest Self; baggage that we carry with us for several generations: going forward on our life path, existing, being unique, experiencing clarification and following the rhythm... rhythm or cycle.

Feet allow us to go forward on our life path, our destiny. Their symbolism is identical to THAT of the key. Our feet give us the power to move on and explore; to make real. Shoes cover our feet and Sandals also dress our feet while allowing them to see... the Sky. Sandals are a symbol that your Soul might use, for example, to show your openness to the Heavenly world, while attending to Earthly concerns. Sandals give wings to your feet and they have been worn for a very long time...

Learning to interpret symbols that your sub*conscious* uses is another key for opening the front door of your own evolution. Discovering what is buried in your un-*conscious* is to discover a priceless treasure. When I was very young, I knew there was a way to use much more of our potential. Through the un-*conscious*, your un-*conscious* and the collective un-*conscious*, you can access a wealth of information, if not *All* the information you have access to, since *All* you have seen, heard and learned is buried there in your un-*conscious*. This is true for *All* of us. What everyone has seen, felt, heard, learned or thought is there in the collective un-*conscious*. Our personal un-*conscious* stops where the collective un-*conscious* begins. And at the limit of the personal un-*conscious* and the collective un-*conscious* are our various archetypes. What are you waiting for then to start exploring? As you discover your "Self" you begin to become *aware* of the "Self".

Personal Applications

In this chapter we are looking at the un-*conscious*; the double aspect of the un-*conscious*. The un-*consciousness* of a person and also everything that is not fully *conscious*. Here we are in the presence of a person who experiences very large karmas. She experiences situations that repeat over several lives. The worst is that she is completely un-*conscious* of it. Someone vibrating in a vortex of negative energy will play the role of the "Super-Mum", "Super-Dad", or "eternal bachelor". She will be lacking greatly in maturity; an eternal teenager. Egocentrism is her main focus. Furthermore, this type of person prefers to live in extreme isolation... if and of course only if, there are emotional blockages. Otherwise, a person vibrating positive energy will be available for others. Maternal or paternal qualities are present in a balanced way. This kind of person is in contact with Souls; non-embodied Souls that are still close to Earth. She will experience a union with a Soul, whether an embodied Spirit or not. Eventually, she will also experience a union with two Souls or Spirits, incarnated or not; *All* according to her contract, a contract she now recognizes. She invites you to her home. She welcomes you. She relates to you. She now realizes she can access everything that is un-*conscious* and that what happens to her was orchestrated before her incarnation. She knows with certainty that there is much, much more beyond death. She lives peacefully and joyfully in active communication with the beyond!

To determine if there is an emotional blockage in your personal life, I suggest you take the time to answer the following questions honestly:

✓ **Do you feel that there are things that recur constantly in your life?**

Do you have recurring dreams or nightmares?

Do you experience recurring events that are very similar? For example: conflicts in your relationships, couple relationships, relationships in general. Do you tend to get involved with the same kind of person in the end?

These are small signs that life is sending you to help you realize there is something that you must set to rights. The goal here is *awareness*. *Consciousness* is the beginning of healing, because once you become *aware* of something, you will notice whenever it resurfaces in your life. And, with time POOF! It will disappear! Like magic! As if by enchantment!

So, play the enchanted magician. I suggest you take a few minutes to think about the signs that life is sending you. Take note if there are any similar events in your life that recur frequently. If you do not notice any recurring patterns in your everyday life, like in your sleep at night, then ask life to kindly send you day signs or night signs and spread them out over several days... the signs you receive may not be served on a silver platter... you will also need to make an effort ... the main objective is to find the link between the various signs which will lead you to the basic message. So, go ahead my little Columbos...

Here is an example. At the beginning of my career as a Soul *Awakener*, I was wondering about my methods. I wondered if what I was receiving was ok. That night, I dreamed that I was receiving messages from God through Angels and Archangels. In the morning, when I woke up, I walked barefoot around inside the house and found mySelf with bird droppings on the tips of my toes. I had two birds in a cage at that time and I had never walked in excrement before. This was *All* for the good, because excrement is synonymous with GOLD. It is the final product of what we have swallowed. In my case, it is the assimilation of what I have learned. Droppings on the tips of my toes meant that I was advancing on my life path as I should be. Furthermore, birds are symbols of Heavenly messages. In other words, my signs helped me recognize that I was re-transmitting exactly the messages that God was sending me for my clients' evolution, thanks to the Angels and Archangels.

✓ Do you tend to be a "Super-Mom" "Super-Dad" or "eternal bachelor"?

If so, then you are excessive. You are not balanced. To re-balance the chakra *connected* to these excesses, I suggest you envisage an energy ball about forty-five centimeters above your head ... touch it with your hands... feel the warmth of this chakra... This chakra is called: "Gate of the Soul", it is medium blue lilac in colour, according to Élias Wolf in the book: *Le Livre des 28 chakras*. By touching it, you can feel, see, hear what you must feel, see and hear in order to re-balance your chakra... remain in this state of communion with the chakra... imagine yourSelf being more available but simply playing your role as father or mother without any excess on your part... not too much, not too little... just as it should be... you can also take this opportunity to come into contact with non-embodied Souls if you want to, since this chakra is the chakra of mediumship. With time and practice, you will be able to exploit these avenues. You may repeat the exercises as you see fit and as often as you like.

✓ Do you tend to believe that you are like others?

Do you refuse to believe you are *unique*?

We are *All unique* individuals. Nobody is exactly like anyone else. We may share features with another person, but the similarities stop there. We are *All* here to learn. However, the difference lies in the lessons that we are here to learn over the course of our lives. Furthermore, most of us are not in our first incarnation, which also makes us different at this level. The base is the same, our Heavenly Father, the Father is the same, but we remain *unique* beings that have evolved from life to life, bringing our baggage along with us. Like the branches on a tree, each branch is *unique*. *All* trees are *connected* to the Earth and the Sun; Mother Earth and Father Sun. Trees live because of the Sun and the Earth. They gave birth to the trees, but each tree has its own family which makes each branch *unique*. You too are *unique*, since you are a branch of a branch of another branch of your family tree...! Do you still believe you are not *unique*?

✓ **Uniting *All* parts of the Self**

This chapter is about the Union of the interior couple, the feminine and masculine parts, the interior father and mother, Light and darkness. And it is also about the Union of three interior parts, for example: for a woman, the inner child, mother and Goddess or for a man, the inner child, father and God...

Do you feel the need to unite parts of yourSelf? Are you experiencing conflict and internal dis-*harmony*? As if a part of you wanted to go to the left, for example, and another to the right.

If so, then I suggest you imagine yourSelf as the intermediary between your parts. You are the mediator. Ask your different parts clearly, one by one, what they really want to say. Be neutral. Listen and write down the discussion on a piece of paper. If you want, ask them questions and write down what they tell you... Stay in a neutral position, do not judge, do not criticize, just listen carefully. Reach a compromise between the different parts of yourSelf in harmony and then unite them. You must first obtain their agreement. If they say yes, proceed as you see fit. Otherwise, ask them the reason for the refusal. There must still be conflicts, so rework the issues with them. If there is no conflict, ask for more details, but do not force anything. The reason may be more complicated... I recommend repeating the exercise another day and asking for more details on the subject. Let it sit for a few days, and then repeat the exercise.

N.B. When the Union happens, include a little celebration. Light a candle and say a prayer. Remember to thank the parts of yourSelf for the experience you have had, regardless of the outcome.

Chapter 19

THE *CONSCIOUS*
☼

The Dawn is now upon us. Golden yellowish-orange colours are in the sky. The Sun rises. It is the beginning of en*light*enment and the end of ignorance. The innocence of the child is his greatest power of *All*: Love, Beauty, Light and Truth. This is the healing and liberating of parts that were imprisoned and smothered in the un-*conscious*.

We are now at the Arcanum of wonderment... a child's wonder. We are full of joy and wonder for life with hearts as pure as a child's... our inner child... and the wisdom of our grandparents.

Arcanum 19 is The Sun which calls for en*light*enment. We have passed over the many satisfactions of the senses. We are now called upon to share spiritual nourishment with our brothers and sisters on Earth. We are called upon to share life's secrets. Temptation is always there, but we now know something else. There is pleasure beyond that provided by the five senses. Success is ours. A life filled with abundance. Life's energy is transported and it nourishes us with great strength, but it is in-*visible* to those still in the shadows. Protection and prediction help us on the path of destiny.

The inner child is One of the archetypes discussed in this chapter; the innocence, wonder and joy of the child that also covets wealth, wisdom and experience. Experience in a form of Love, never experienced before. This is a Love so great that sex is nothing; an androgynous Love since the inner man and woman are now ONE. A radiant being, shinning with *All* its power. The test and initiation... have now been proven. Divine Light sends rays of *know*ledge and joy. We receive energy from the Sky and also the Earth and we give it back to our brothers and sisters. However, we must still spend a few moments of solitude to allow our Soul to center itself and to integrate. This energy, this great power was transmitted to us through a major inner cleaning. Cleaning of what was previously obscure at the un-*conscious* level. The result allows us to be happy and filled with purity and *All* in total *Consciousness*.

The Source of our healing is God; Love, *unconditional* Love, Peace, Joy, Trust and Faith... great Faith in God. We have undergone an Internal cleaning of our old wounds. We are now open to our Higher *Consciousness*... and we are going toward greater Wisdom. However, we still have three small Laws to pass through before achieving the greatest Wisdom of *All*. The Law in question here is the Law of Polarity; after night comes day, after death, birth... or rather re-birth!

The Arcanum, The Sun is related to the seventh astrological house, and therefore marriages, partners and unions... Union is a sign of great stability and abundance in our lives. A human being who works with Celestial and Earthly forces tends towards his own evolution. The unfertilized egg is a symbol of Universal chaos. The rainbow is the alliance between humans and the great forces of the Cosmos. The table symbolizes stability, unity and abundance, and if it is covered with food when it is overturned, then it is the sign of a broken marriage. If there are any eggs on the table and the table is overturned and an egg is broken, then it signifies inner relief. *All* that work is done with the help of our Guides. There is communication with the Spirit of infinite intelligence. A new life purified of our past experiences; the empty glass. You remember, in chapter 14, the voice I heard that predicted the birth of a child. Well, this is it.

Communicate with the *visible* and in-*visible* world. Listen to what Guides and Spirits have to say. Learn to recognize your own Soul families. Where you come from and where you are going to... Getting to know your real Self... To be informed... No longer from the outside to the inside, but rather from the inside to the outside... This is the song of life!

Personal Applications

In this chapter, *All* the attention is put on *Consciousness*; *Consciousness* in *All* its wonder. Live *conscientiously*, at least that is what we are trying to achieve! We pass from the un-*consciousness* of night to the *consciousness* of day. Then, if that is our Divine plan, we will go to the great *consciousness*; the west to east axis is of great importance in our daily lives. The Sun rises in the east and sets in the west. The Law of Polarity illustrates the balance of life, *consciousness*, un-*consciousness*, day, night, work, rest... A person who vibrates in a vortex of negative energy will play the role of the so-called healer and will practice spirituality in solitude. This kind of person will be in conflict with God, she will be the greatest of rebels. Her radiance will be very limited, since her spiritual journey is not shared... if and of course only if, there are emotional blockages. Otherwise, a person vibrating positive energy will play the role of a healer of Light, in other words, she is a medium of Light and not darkness like she used to be. She will radiate a great spiritual Light that will allow a Union with the Masters or her Soul family. She will be in contact with Light beings and Guides. She knows how to get help from in-*visible* forces. She is supported from above. She gets help from Guides. She recognizes her resemblance to other Spirits. She communicates from Soul to Soul. She recognizes the needs of the Soul. And *All* of this, with joy and simplicity!

To determine if there is an emotional blockage in your personal life, I suggest you take the time to answer the following questions honestly:

✓ **Do you often feel sad?**

Do you lose feelings of *joy* quickly?

If so, then I suggest you pay attention to the times when you have lost the thread of *joy*. Can you compare these moments with those when you were *happier*? Notice what's wrong... What brought you into this state? Is it because of words you may have heard? Is it from the past? A movie you saw? An emotion you experienced? What happened exactly? Why are you like this? Make these observations for at least three situations in which you have experienced sadness... Then compare your experiences... What are the differences? What are the similarities? Then ask aloud what is the Source of *All* your moments of sadness... you may receive an answer in symbolic form... a colour... a smell... a sound... a song... a word... a special taste... Your goal is to uncover the meaning of this message... What does this symbol mean to you? What is your Soul trying to tell you exactly? You may not be well *connected* to it, since you live in a kind of dis-harmony. Maybe your Soul has recognized something that you have already experienced in another life... So, from now on you know the Sources of your sadness and this will allow you to be *aware* in the future. You will be *aware* of the Sources before sinking into sadness in the future.

If you wish, you can repeat the exercise for other times when you have had similar experiences. The more you know about your Sources of sadness, the more you will be able to prevent them from occurring in the future.

Then, I would ask you to make a list of images, words, sounds, music, songs and emotions that make you *happy* and feed your *joy*. Any form of *joy* is welcome on your list. Write down everything that is *wonderful* to you. Then remember a sad situation you experienced, but this time, see it a few minutes before the emotion of sadness arises... then as soon as you realize that you are sinking into sadness, change the situation by recalling one of the items on your list of *joy*. You are stopping the sadness before it grows and in its place you experience a memory that brings you great *joy*. Repeat this exercise as often as you wish. The more you repeat it, the more it becomes a habit. A very good habit!

Music and singing, for example, are also excellent ways to ward off any Source of negativity. Listening to music or singing regularly with others repels sadness. Personally, I managed to change my way of thinking by singing. If, for example, I had a negative thought or emotion, I would sing. With time and practice, I sang without having any negative thoughts or emotions and they totally disappeared from my life. It is quite logical, since I now vibrate in a vortex of positive energy, so there is no more room for negative energy.

N.B   An Black Obsidian stone gives *great joy* and a lot of *happiness*. However, if you do not respect it, it will cause you to experience great sadness and worse...

✓ **Do you often experience strong emotional feelings, as though you were *connected* to *All* emotion in the rest of the world?**

If so, then you probably have extra-sensory perception and are empathetic. You can definitely feel the emotions and discomforts of others. To be sure of this, next time you experience it, I suggest you ask who the emotion belongs to. Ask if it is yours. So next time you feel emotion or an discomfort, especially if it is an un-familiar emotion or discomfort, simply ask if it is yours. If it is not, it will disappear and if it is, it will stay. If it stays, ask to understand its Source. When you understand it, return it to its Source. Imagine it going back to its Source surrounded by a beautiful white Light.

A lot of people are empathetic (kinaesthetic). In fact, empathy is the most exploited gift. If you find you have the gift to feel what others may be experiencing and you want to protect yourSelf, here are several tips for you.

Sea salt has the ability to absorb negativity and soothe you. You can use it in different ways. Add a pinch of sea salt to your bath water, and then soak in it for a few minutes. Bury small bags of sea salt around your property and at the four corners of the property to protect it. Hang small bags of Himalayan salt from the top corners of your doors; this will protect the interior of your home. You can even put small plates of sea salt on the floor at the four corners of your bed. This will protect you at night when you are sleeping. Change the salt regularly, flushing it down the toilet. There are also several types of lamps made from Himalayan salt that you can put wherever you like around your house and even in your office. I have several lamps in my house and office. Recently, I bought a small salt lamp with a USB connection for the computer in my office; it eliminates negative waves emitted by the screen thereby promoting energy in the room.

Music is also a good way to protect yourSelf wherever you are, even at night when you are asleep. If you are an insomniac, for example, you can put on relaxation music that promotes sleep and this kind of music will keep negative energy away.

You can also use stones to protect yourSelf. Black Tourmaline, Turquoise, Malachite and Black Jasper are good examples of protective stones. In addition, you can use the help of the Archangel Michael to protect you if you wish. His mission is protection, so he will respond to your request as soon as you ask him. In fact, *All* the Angels and Archangels can protect you.

Saint-Germain is also a great Source of protection with his beautiful purple flame. You only have to invoke the purple flame, see it and feel it inside you, for example, and it will accomplish its mission of protection. I have been protecting mySelf with it for several years. I see it in me, a bit above the heart chakra, at the level of the thymus chakra and I see it spreading throughout my entire body. I carry out this ritual every morning. And I know it really works, because I have had the chance to test it in the past. One day, I met a Feng Shui teacher who could simply see into a person's life by touching his or her aura. However, he could not see anything in mine. I knew it was because I was protected by the purple flame. Therefore, I use it whenever I feel the need. This is one of the easiest tools I use and does not require any special equipment, so it can be used anywhere.

Frankincense (incense) is also a good tool for protection, especially if you are cleaning, healing, or if you have clients who come into your office. It purifies the environment and stimulates certain things depending on the type of incense used. Sage is the incense of choice for purification, harmonization and protection. Use dried sage leaves and not sage sticks, they only perfume the environment.

Candles are also a great Source of protection. They remove impurities in the air. Furthermore, thanks to their use, you can see the toxins that are eliminated by the smoke they make. You can also see the energy in the room. If the flame of your candle is moving and there is no airflow, you know you have visitors. When you combine incense and candles, you create a double protection or purification in your environment. Therefore, when you do *entity or energy cleaning*[4] in your home or elsewhere, you can use sage, sea salt and candles, this way you can see if there are any entities in your home.

☆·.,.·´¯`·.,.¤ ~ ๏ °

---

[4]   Procedure to clean negative energy or entities in your environment. Put sea salt on the floor in every corner of every room. Leave the salt three full days. Then, at the end of the third day, remove the salt with a dustpan and dispose of it in the toilet. (The salt must be eliminated in a Source of running water.) Then visualize a channel of light from the center of the earth up to the celestial Source through the center of your home. Go into each room, one by one, light a candle in the middle of the room and brush the air with sage smoke praying and asking the energy or entity to leave your home, say that you are the owner and you do not want it in your house anymore and speak firmly. Tell it that you are protected by God and it must leave. Tell it to leave either by a window or a door (open the door or window of each room when you enter and leave them open until the very end of the procedure) or it can go into the light. Tell it there is nothing to be afraid of and that is where it is supposed to go. Then, repeat this process for each room. When you are finished, close the channel by thanking Light beings, guides, angels, archangels, God and any entities that were willing to return to the light. Then blow out the candles and close the doors and windows if you wish. The energy of your house is now purified. Repeat the procedure when you feel the need. If you have an office where you receive clients, then I advise you to clean it like this, often.

Chapter 20

RE-INCARNATION

♥

The previous card showed the beginning of *awakening*, dawn, East, the majestic eagle. Now, this Arcanum called Judgment, represents the *true awakening*! Noon, South, Great serpent... This is the final step towards "Self" realization. The energy of the Soul vibrates at a higher frequency at the level of spiritual desires rather than material ones. At this point, the individual is considered part of the whole, separation no longer figures in his existence.

Judgment is the twentieth Arcanum in tarot; it refers to the great power of forgiveness, forgiveness of ourselves, others and events. The individual now knows that he has incarnated to learn and that *All* he has lived is part of his experience, so he agrees. Forgiveness is the only way to wisdom. We have agreed to let the past die and to start on a new level here and now. Thus, we are participating in our re-incarnation under the influence of the eighth astrological house which affects everything representing the depths, near or far; the depths of our own inner selves. Free yourSelf of your inner God of opinion. Trust that everything that happens to you is for the best and manifest the "Law of Compensation". Compensation or compassion...

The archetype related to this Arcanum is the judge. The judge, acting as mediator, will lean towards a balance between justice and compassion. The predominant characteristics of this archetype are justice and wisdom. Often, individuals affected by this archetype have been misjudged in the past and have greatly suffered and they have had to learn to forgive. So that is what makes them excellent mediators. However, if they work with their darker side, negative criticism and judgment are used to manipulate and abuse, abuse their power and authority. Will you condemn an old lady who stole a loaf of bread to feed her grandchildren? Who are we to judge the actions of others, we know absolutely nothing of their lives anyway and "everyone always makes the best decision in the present moment according to their *know*ledge", isn't it so, my NLP friends?

We are therefore asked to change the way we conduct our lives. Sometimes it is necessary to dig up the dead to re-orient ourselves on our life path, the path that suits us, the Divine Plan. We must open our eyes and see where life wants to take us. While I was studying this Arcanum, I dreamed that I was baptized. The symbol of immersion means purification and re*new*al. According to the dictionary of symbols, baptism has two actions or phases: immersion and emersion. "Although immersion may now be reduced to sprinkling with water, bears a wealth of meaning in itself – the sinful creature vanishing in the waters of death, purification by lustration and the revitalization of that creature from the source of life. Emersion reveals the purified being in a state of grace, united with a divine stream of new life." *Dictionary of Symbols,* Jean Chevalier and Alain Gheerbrant. Emersion is the phase of baptism that speaks the most to me, because I saw mySelf in a waterfall that was flowing from a chain of rocks. This reflects the re-birth of my Divine part. I re-Source directly to the Source of *All*! And that is really what I feel now, while I am writing this book! Furthermore, the meaning of my name Chantal is rock. I could not be closer to my Source!

While studying the previous Arcanum, the Sun, I read a book on Soul families. When I read the book, I recognized my own Soul family: "The Alchemist-Fairy!" It was easy to associate mySelf with this Soul family, even though I recognized a bit of mySelf in *All* the groups. Transformation, cleaning, purification, angelic energy, lightness, difficulty integrating the physical body... "To spiritualize the material world" is what I am here to teach through multiple forms of communication. Please note, the fairies are actually nature Angels and that is why I prefer the countryside, water, mountains and animals to the city and its pollution. I was a technician in analytical chemistry for more than ten years. My last job was at Safety-Kleen where toxic waste is recycled. Furthermore, by chance, the fairy's mission is to help preserve the environment and protect *All* its small inhabitants, plants, trees, water, animals...

Live in the present moment and re-*new* yourSelf. Undo the ties of the past and delete old, poorly recorded records. We have small disks inside, small wheels of energy called chakras; Energy in-*visible* to the human eye that records information and continues to do so, which is why we are eternal beings. This energy, this accumulation of information follows our Soul from its conception and will continue to do so long after our transformation, the transformation of our vehicle, our physical body, the temple of our Soul. Thus, daily harmonization of the chakras, good nutrition, adequate rest, drinking plenty of water, for example, gives us access to this information and we can modify it, if necessary, in our quest for Self-realization.

Sometimes we experience anxieties, fantasies, fears... They are ghosts of the past coming back to haunt us! To regain our own power, we must cut some sequences from the film of our existence. You have only to ask the Archangel Michael to help you with that ONE. He will be happy to help you cut etheric links that *connect* you to a person, group of people, animals, things and events that drain your energy or send negative energy to you. You will feel the Archangel Michael around you during the process and you may even be able to see him... if you see a beautiful royal blue Light it is him!

Personal Applications

In this chapter, we are talking about being *aware* that we are re*new*ing every second of our existence. Say goodbye to the past and move forward on your path, living for the present moment. The "Law of Reincarnation" illustrates re*new*al and re-birth and the fact that, every day, we are on the road returning home. We are returning to the Source... A person who vibrates in a vortex of negative energy will play the role of the betrayer or the lost one. This kind of person moves forward, completely un-*aware* of her own path. She fails every step of the way in her life. She wants to be special and her greatest desire is to succeed, regardless of the cost... if and of course only if, there are emotional blockages. Otherwise, a person vibrating positive energy will play the role of Guide, the one who prepares the path. She will possess considerable charisma. She lives life to the fullest right to the tip of her toes. She has an ordinary character, but with *All* that is honourable. She knows lawfully how things should be. She recognizes her own place in the Universe. She feels the direction of her life path. She greets her vocation. She lives and brings her offerings. She remains faithful. She has the loyalty of a person who is not lost and understands why she is incarnated each and every day that God allows her to continue on her road to destiny!

To determine if there is an emotional blockage in your personal life, I suggest you take the time to answer the following questions honestly:

✓ **Are you _aware_ that you re-_new_ yourSelf every second?**

If I told you that every cell in our body is re_new_ed every moment, would you agree that we also re-_new_ at every moment?

Re_new_al means replace with something else so that today is different from yesterday and tomorrow will be different from today. The days pass and there are no two days alike. Thus, today is different from yesterday and tomorrow will also be different from today... Now, what do you think, do you believe you re-_new_ every moment?

✓ **Now, do you believe in _re-incarnation_?**

What is the difference between you and your cells?

There is no difference is there? You are your cells and your cells are you? When I say that your cells die and are _re-born_ each moment it is the phenomenon of dead skin or wound healing for example, these are examples of the death and _re-birth_ of cells. So if cells in the physical body can change, why couldn't you? You are your cells and your cells are you! What is the difference?

✓ **Do you know your _vocation_?**

Do you know your own _path_?

Do you know your _life purpose_?

Why do you think you were incarnated?

If you do not know your _life purpose_, your _life mission_ or if you need additional information, I suggest you do the following exercise. Stand up and stretch your arms upwards, reaching to the Sky above your head. You will feel energy at your fingertips, a ball of energy. This ball of energy is the "vocation chakra". I would ask you to kindly remain in this position for a few moments, eyes closed... Imagine a ball that is coloured a shade of blue interspersed in equal quantities with a Light golden greenish shade ... say the following statements out loud: "I now recognize my *life path*", "My *vocation* is now welcome in my life". Then wait to receive a message, sign or symbol and remain in this position for a few moments... during this time, your body and you will re-new... you may not receive any message immediately, you may receive one over the next few days or weeks, either during the day or through dreams at night, but do not worry, you will receive messages soon. If you do not receive any messages about your *vocation* and *life mission*, then ask to be guided in this direction in the coming days... wait a few minutes, then slowly open your eyes... you can repeat this exercise whenever you wish, it permits you to receive the information you need about your *life path*!

I suggest you write the statements down and put them in a place where you will see them as often as possible during the day. And if you can, repeat them as frequently as possible. You can use these affirmations: "I now recognize my *life path*", "my *vocation* is welcome in my life now" or you can create new ones. However, you must write them in a positive way. Be precise and write in the present tense. For example, you cannot write: "I do not want to gain weight". This statement will be understood by your brain as: "I want to gain weight ". In fact the negation is not understood. It is as if the word 'not' was omitted in the sentence, as if it was only reading the important words. Write instead: "I am thin." Also, when you say affirmations or other forms of demands really live them, feel them, hear them, taste them and enjoy every moment of this experience. This allows you to receive faster, because it is as if you were already there. That is why Jesus was a Master in the art of being present, he knew the Laws of how to receive. He said that with practice, we would be able to receive the crops before harvest time, as he knew so well. So create. On your marks, get set... ready? Go!

✓ **In what way are you un*faith*ful?**

Do you feel that you are betraying a code of honour?

What moral principles do you dis-honour?

The word infidel originates from the Latin word *infidelis*, which means ''unreliable'', according to Antidote. So, in the nuance of these writings, in what way do you feel you are un*trust*worthy?

The word unworthy means among other things, not worthy. The belief that we are not deserving comes from far away... The archetype of the slave expresses it. The servant is also an archetype that may tend to believe he does not deserve. The priest, monk and nun take vows and therefore forego certain privileges. The Messiah, the Redeemer, the Saviour are *All* archetypes that have had to give up certain privileges in the past. If you have one or more of these archetypes that do not deserve, then you may still experience this energy in this life. That is why you still believe you do not deserve...

P.S.   For more information on the archetypes, see *Sacred Contracts* by Caroline Myss.

I suggest you perform a purification of your crystallized archetypes that make you feel dis-*loyal*, dis-*honourable* or un-*worthy*. Next time you take a bath, add sea salt to it. Let the water run until you are immersed in it and can stretch out. Live your emotion (un-*faith*ful, dis-*loyal*, dis-*honourable*, un-*worthy*...) and feel it in your body. Then move the emotion to your heart, if it was not already there. Open your heart to feel (un-*faithful*, dis-*loyal*, dis-*honourable*, un-*worthy*, un-*deserving*...) and see it filled with Love, Compassion and Peace. Feel the deep understanding in your body now and say goodbye to that negative feeling. Say thank you and ask it to return to its Source. Now you understand its origin and its presence in your life. Watch it go from your heart to its Source surrounded by a beautiful emerald green Light. Do the exercise three times per bath, one bath a day and for three days in a row. You can use a candle and incense while taking your bath. I also suggest you seek assistance from your Guides, Angels, Archangels, or other Spirits as you wish.

Chapter 21

THE RE-COGNITION

All the elements are united. The snake is also included. The final piece of the puzzle is being placed. This is a crucial moment... the realization. We are witnessing the creation of a great work; perfection, the Union of the Soul with the entire Universe. A cycle is finally completed.

The World is the twenty-first Arcanum in tarot; it is associated with the tenth astrological house, reputation, career, success, in relation to the mother... A positive affirmation that generates from this Arcanum is: "I accomplish successfully everything that I undertake". It is a statement that I have been using for a very long time, as long as I can remember. There are beliefs and values with which we were born, I think, and this is one of mine. In my heart, I always knew that no matter what I did, I would always succeed and even more... It is a belief that I do not want to change in anyway. It allowed me to be who I am today. It allowed me to be part of the best, of course, when I wanted.

The Law referred to in this chapter is the "Law of Correspondence"; Correspondence, origins, roots, Sources which is very logical, because the Arcanum is called The World. Studying correspondences is a part of my life path and of great interest to me. In metaphysics, we always try to understand where the problem, sickness or disease comes from, in other words its Source. A physical illness demands a physical treatment, because negative energy has successfully touched the physical being. But you will probably treat and re-treat the sore constantly, if you do not find its Source. As if you were only trimming the weeds instead of uprooting them... Here, among others, we can see the need for the "Law of Correspondence". I received a client in my office who told me that doctors could not understand why his heart was beating so slowly and yet he still managed to live normally. We discussed this matter in my office for about an hour and a half to find the Source of his dis-ease. He looked at himSelf in the mirror and saw a dead man. I gave him some homework: he had to look at himSelf in the mirror as often as possible and compliment himSelf. After a few weeks, his energy had completely changed. He shines now. I felt, saw and heard what I had to feel, see and hear at that moment to open up his *consciousness*, to bring un-*conscious* behaviours into *consciousness*. The un-*conscious* is only responding to the orders it receives. In this case, the command was "death"! It took us only an hour and a half to pull out the weeds. As a Coach, if you do not go down to the roots (the Source), you may continue watering the weeds, when the ultimate goal is to help your client grows wings!

The Law of Correspondence is also related to communication. Synchronization is a great way to communicate and hear what the Soul wants to say, to be on the same wave length as the other. When we are at the same frequency, we are equal and communication takes place more easily. We are *All* inter*connected*, so it is normal that we receive for each other. I communicate with the Spirit World. I see, hear and feel what I have to see, hear and feel in the present moment, for the evolution and healing of the greatest number of people. However, to receive messages from God, we must first have recognized our negative origins, our darker roots. God is a Light being and to be an intermediary between Him and his creatures, we must have transformed our dark side or at least be able to put it aside while transmitting, channelling and receiving... otherwise, you will not get anything very, very Bright! However, this is probably what must be, so... let it be, let it be! ♪♪♪

The Arcanum the World is generally associated with a humanitarian energy: the olive tree, symbol of peace, wealth, fertility and reward. We have to overcome our internal dualities for the victory of this great battle. It is the end of the sex wars to finally return home and find the comfort and safety of our own homes: the energy of the protective mother who provides security. The Spiritual home. The temple. Love, Peace, Well-being and Joy... Sources of happiness. Swim in the water and play with the fishes...

We are Light beings, Love beings. Healing helps heal our collective energy, because we are inter*connected*. So we *All* swim in the same water. And if you heal, the water becomes less and less contaminated. The goal is not to wait until the apple is rotten, but to help preserve it, if that is its destiny.

While I was studying this Arcanum, I came to understand the Source of my in-*security* in this world through the analysis of a dream I had. Although I am the oldest in my family, I am the second in the family; my mother had a miscarriage just before becoming pregnant with me. My Soul has tried to be the first, but it was as if it had no choice but to be the second; as if the project was aborted at the last minute, or rather rejected. I now understand a bit better why it takes me a while to finish my projects. I am often missing something to complete it... but I do finish it finally. Maybe not with first place, but among the best!

When I am working in the garden, I am in my element. It is a form of therapy for me. I am closer to the Earth, to Mother-

Earth. I hold her in my hands. Channels open up and I receive a lot. Often, when we take the time to do something different, we find solutions; as if by letting go, we receive more and more. Isn't it true that often once we stop looking for something, we find it! We can believe we are at the right place, at the right time and then life takes us somewhere else, elsewhere, on a purer and brighter path. We *All* have the capacity to take the path of our destiny, to follow the road that shows us our heart. Love is the Source of *All*! Forget the play in which you play a role you do not like. The only role you must play is the ONE you Love. Doing the opposite of what your heart tells you is wrong. So... you reap what you sow! We are talking about the truest possible in-*fidelity* in *All* reality!

Personal Applications

This chapter is about being *aware* that we are on the right path, the ONE that calls us toward the success of our undertakings and also calls us to a higher level which is the World. We are finally re-cognized in the world, because we are following our own life path. In general, this is not the usual. Usually everyone follows everyone else like sheep, but that is not part of the scenery here. Instead we have a person who has followed a tortuous and unusual path. This is a person with great courage and Self confidence. The end of the project is near; it will soon be accomplished and made real. The efforts of the journey will soon be rewarded... A person who vibrates negative energy will play the biggest fanatic and the smallest blasphemer. This is a rebellious person, living in conflict with God whom he blames for everything and nothing. This kind of person is not master of his own behaviour. Control is not part of his life. He does not feel responsible for anything. He is always on the defensive and defends everything and nothing. He could experience moments of extreme Self esteem that might lead to some form of arrogance... if and of course only if, there are emotional blockages. Otherwise, a person who vibrates positive energy will play the role of servant and Sage, servant of God and her Soul and not of the Ego. This person will be in personal contact with God our Heavenly Father. She lives a life of contemplation, in the greatest simplicity and humility. She is held by the Divine. She lives a life of perfection and magnificence. She is ONE with *All*. She is ONE with God the Father. She serves. She channels Love, Peace, Joy, Light and Truth!

To determine if there is an emotional blockage in your personal life, I suggest you take the time to answer the following questions honestly:

✓ **Are you the servant of your Soul or your Ego?**

Your Soul is the part of you that directs you on your life path, while your Ego directs you on the path of the material world. Material, fear, pain, dis-ease, individualism... are *All* words in the vocabulary of the Ego. This dark side of you wants you to believe that you are separate from the rest of the world, while your Soul works to unite you with the rest of humanity. It is the generous, compassionate, gentle and loving part of yourSelf. At no time would it try to make you feel, guilt, shame, rage, anger or anxiety... to name just a few emotions created by Mr. Ego. The aim of the Soul is to work in harmony with you so that you radiate with *All* your Lights!

So, are you the servant of your Soul or your Ego?

I suggest you close your eyes and imagine a star about two meters above your head. The star is a dark purple bluish colour, surrounded by beautiful golden sparks. Feel and see a flame inside you now. This flame is your Soul. It could be located just above your chest. Feel your flame located at the thymus chakra about midway between the throat and the heart chakra. The thymus chakra is turquoise, it is a secondary chakra. Now see and feel your inner flame extend throughout your body from your thymus down into your chest, your stomach, your hips, your legs, your thighs, into your lap, your calves, your ankles, your feet and through your toes... then from your thymus up to your shoulders, arms, elbows, hands and into the tips of your fingers then your neck and your head. See and feel your Soul leave your head, knowing that you are grounded to the

Earth... the flame goes to the star which is about two meters above your head and unites the flame with the star... the star is your star... when the unification has happened you can see the dark purple bluish star surrounded by beautiful golden sparks, ONE with your inner flame... stay in this position for a few moments so that you can understand, see, hear, feel or perceive the goodness of being united with an energy of Love, Peace, Joy, Light and Truth! Then see the flame returning to your physical body knowing that you are now united with your "Celestial Star". Bring with you *All* the Love, Peace, Joy, Light and Truth you need for the present moment. Then, taking *All* the time in the world, come back, here and now, in the next second!

✓ **Do you *achieve* want you want?**

If not...

If someone saw you now, how would he or she describe you? Describe yourSelf as seen through the eyes of someone else.

Now you come to life more fully. You *realize* your dreams and desires. So, describe yourSelf as seen through the eyes of someone else. How do others see you at present?

What are the differences?

What is the next step you need to *accomplish* today, so you can fully *realize* one of your dreams or desires? Take the time to think about it and when your decision is made, commit yourSelf to this first step. Take one step at a time, baby steps, but go ahead. *Realization* allows us to grow and flourishing makes you shine. Through our en*light*enment we are a Source of inspiration for others. Thus, we contribute to the Well-being, Love, Joy and Light of humanity.

✓ **Would you like to be able to *channel*?**

If so, I suggest you try the method I use to open my *channel*. This "way" is mine. It is not a rule or a Truth, it is my Truth and it may be not yours, but I will still share it with you so you can try it. After, feel free to find your own...

I sit comfortably, eyes closed, and I sing "OM" (which is a spiritual sound). To do this, I put on a CD with the song "OM" in the background. I start singing the "O" by visualizing energy beneath my feet, from the crystal in the center of the Earth, energy from Mother-Earth. Energy filled with Love, Security, Creativity, Abundance, Protection and Confidence... I see and feel the energy, Light, heat, going up through roots beneath my feet. I feel the energy entering through the soles of my feet, moving in my legs, through my knees, then up to my buttocks and it goes through my coccyx, and from there, I see and feel the energy that passes through my root chakra (located at the base of the spinal column, above the tailbone, its colour is red) and then, through my sacral chakra (ten centimetres above the root chakra, its colour is orange) and then, through the solar plexus chakra (located halfway between the navel and the breastbone, its colour is yellow) and finally, through the heart chakra (located at the heart level, but centered, its colour is emerald green). Then I take a deep breath into my abdomen and always through my nose, and I sing the "M" (the sound "M" is made with the mouth closed and teeth almost touching ... the goal is to raise the liquid of the glands in the head. The longer your "M" vibrates, the better the results and it is proven that it brings more Joy) visualizing the energy continuing its journey to the throat chakra (located at the level of the throat, its colour is blue) and then going up to the head. Here I see the energy spreading into my head, through the third eye chakra (located between the two physical eyes at the level of the eyebrows, its colour is indigo blue), ears chakra (located on each side the head in an angle of 45 degrees from the temples, its colour is a pale bluish purple), to the back of the head and forehead, and then out of my skull from the top, that is to say, through the crown chakra (located at the middle and top of the head, its colour is purple), and to finally move toward the Father. Star, Sun, Sky, Cosmos... I repeat this sequence several times. I only stop when I feel satisfied. Then I pray for a while (praying for me is not reciting prayers from a specific religion, but rather my own words, thoughts, requests and thanks). Then I start the sequence over again, but this time I sing the "O" in the same way, that is to say, by visualizing the energy coming into my own physical body starting at the Terrestrial Source. However, when I sing "M", I visualize the opposite path, I see the energy coming toward me from the Celestial Source... I open my chakras: Solar plexus (seat of emotions), heart (seat of Love) and thymus (seat of the Soul). I do this procedure three to seven times. Then I start my day, coaching, Soul reading, writing... Thanks to my daily discipline, I now feel the energy flowing through my whole body and as soon as I listen to a CD with the song "OM", I am immediately *connected*. I have been doing this for a couple of years now and it is a great Source of energy for me. This is not the recipe for *All*, but rather my own personal recipe. Now, discover your own recipe!

Chapter 0 or 22

Faith or the Fool

First, we must ask the question: "Are we at the first or the last card in the game?" The Fool is the beginning of creation, the balance of the inner feminine and masculine parts. We are talking about the origin, the Source, the cosmic egg, what is hidden and in-*visible* to most of us.

"Fool through the eyes of men, but wise through the eyes of God"; that is how the Fool in Tarot is represented. He carries a bag containing only a few goods, necessities, memories and *All* his potential in which the Truth is hidden. The Fool, also named Mate, because his name derives from the word "checkmate" wanders peacefully on his path without any worries. He is an active dreamer. The inspired, the initiated and poets are *All* beings that can pass for Fools in the eyes of those who are afraid or do not have the *know*ledge needed to see, See in other ways. Mystery, the un-*known*, imagination are a part of his life.

He is ONE who has a "firm belief" that allows him to continue on his path. He is the perfect model of "healer and channel" because he is always in direct communication with Heaven and Earth. He is the image of a rainbow, a human rainbow. The Fool... consists of *All* the Arcana together. That is why I believe he is the end of this teaching and also the beginning of a new life! A new life that is healed!

His image is like Light piercing a crystal. He is wonder to the mystic... Creativity to the artist... Inspiration to the writer.

They *All* let themselves be penetrated by a "supernatural" energy, just like our friend The Fool, hence his resemblance to a rainbow. He is... the crystal tickled by the sun's rays.

His energy is wisdom, magic, power, innocence, *knowledge* and Light. Zero... symbol of the circle, Divine protection, return... returning to the Source. With the previous Arcanum, we mentioned the snake which was a spiral snake, encircling a man with its head looking toward the sky. Here, the snake (or dragon) is an ouroboros, a snake that forms a circle by eating its own tail. The ouroboros is... the symbol of the perfection of being, the success of a being complete in himSelf. It is the symbol of the interior marriage and the wise man, pure and humble, who has managed to overcome his inner struggles. This is the model of the man who has achieved a perfect balance. This is the man who vibrates in harmony with life. In other words, a man created in the image of God, as God created him... and he sees God in everything and everywhere!

With the previous Arcanum, we were almost at the top of the mountain. After a well deserved break, we have arrived at the summit where we will receive instructions and then share them with our brothers and sisters. In collusion with Divine energy, he teaches the truth and the Laws of the Spirit and he will never go forward by himSelf from now on. He has learned otherwise, that it just simply does not work. He has sacrificed everything to get where he is now.

He is... the disciple who Masters *All* parts of his being, the Saviour, the Messiah, the Hero. He is... under Divine protection. He is... safe from the elements. He goes towards... absolute success. He acts according to... his intuition. He could be the archetype of the Player, because he has "unfailing faith" in his intuition. According to some, he might even be considered a player who risks a lot, since he follows his own path. He takes the path to the left. The road less traveled. He is... the lion and from afar ... the sheep that follows the other sheep.

He expands his gifts. He has learned to re-cognize his emotions and to understand their Source, which is within him, and now he plays with energy. He knows that everything is energy and he has fun discovering new horizons. His goal is to be centered on a single emotion: Love. He vibrates in unison with his Soul and goes forward on his path of destiny; the ONE he has chosen. His aim is to have as much experience as possible. He knows that these experiences teach him new things. At this point, he is... convinced that chance does not exist. Everything happens for a reason, but intuition, not reason, is the solution.

Of course, he may seem Foolish... for those who do not see what he sees... for those who do not feel what he feels... for those who do not understand what he understands... or for someone who is afraid! The Fool knows that fear is only a creation of the Ego. He is no longer afraid; he knows he is a communication medium for God. Thus, he knows that *All* operations are directed by God. To be afraid is the equivalent of not having faith in Him. As Jesus said so well: "Why are ye fearful, oh ye of little faith?" It is as though during my first trip or the first part of my trip, I decided where I wanted to go and then, during my second trip or the second part of my trip, I am going where God wants me to go...

... it is the end

or the beginning...

"Om mani padme hum"

Glossary

ஃ

LIFE PATH OR NUMEROLOGY – The numerology (or life path) of an individual is calculated from his or her date of birth. For example: if you were born January 1, 1981, 01/01/1981, your numerology would be 3, 0+1+0+1+1+9+8+1=21=2+1=3. If you were born June 25, 1966, 06/25/1966 your life path is 0+6+25+1+9+6+6=53/8 and your numerology is 8. For some authors, the Life Path is the sum of all the numbers, keeping the tens so that in the first case it is 21/3 and in the second, 53/8. Other authors will break it down further. Let's take the second example: 0+6+2+5+1+9+6+6=35/8, the numerology is always the final result so here it is 8. Nevertheless, the life path of the person passes through 3 and 5, and then goes to 8. Similarly, in the first example, the life path of the person passes through 2 and 1, and then goes to 3.

PROFESSIONAL CERTIFIED NLP COACH – A Professional Coach in NLP has successfully trained for more than 1000 hours in neuro- linguistic programming with a specialization in Coaching. This training allows an individual to develop and master the techniques and skills of NLP and grants him or her the right to use the title of Professional Certified Coach in NLP.

SOUL AWAKENER – A Soul Awakener is a spiritual Coach. She or he connects directly to the Soul of the other person in all consciousness, and sees, feels and understands... what that Soul wants to express so deeply. A Soul Awakener is someone who works in concert with the Soul of the other, Soul to Soul, bringing awareness to that person of the Soul's existence so that she or he will receive the knowledge needed for his or her evolution, healing and life path... and much, more!

KARMA– Karmic lessons are what we are here to learn about on Earth. These lessons are calculated according to your name. The missing letters in your name are assigned to a lesson, because each letter of the alphabet corresponds to a number and the missing numbers are karmic lessons. For example: Chantal Leduc = 3815213 35433. (Based on the fact that each letter corresponds to a number between 1 and 9, we start with the number 1 for the letter A and we do a Theosophical calculation after 9 (e.g. 10=1+0=1)). In the name Chantal Leduc, the missing numbers are 6, 7 and 9. The number 6 corresponds to *marriage karma*, 7 is related to *faith* and *beliefs*, and 9 is associated with *humanity*.

ORB – Circle of light of variable size attributed, among others, according to some authors, to the presence of light beings, angels or archangels...

NLP – Neuro Linguistic Programming is a study that promotes communication with others and with oneself. It consists of techniques and skills all focused on communication and transformation. These techniques and skills are based on models taken from a variety of people who excelled in their field, such as the therapist Milton H. Erickson, Walt Disney and many more!

YIN – Cosmological principle from Taoist philosophy and complementary to yang, which corresponds to passivity, according to Antidote[5].

---

5   Antidote dictionary

YANG – Cosmological principle from Taoist philosophy and complementary to yin, which corresponds to activity or movement, according to Antidote[6].

---

[6]   Antidote dictionary

▽ △ **Inspiration** △ ▽

Claircognizance

▽ △ Arcana of the Tarot △ ▽

▽ △ The astrological houses △▽:

CONSCIOUS:

HOUSE 1: ASCENDANT: The Self, behaviour, vitality, physical appearance, Ego, personality... of the individual.

HOUSE 2: Money earned and managed, property, appetites, possessions, personal values.

HOUSE 3: Immediate surroundings, brothers and sisters, short trips, small trips, short studies, communication, Self expression.

HOUSE 4: IMUM COELI: Home, family, origins, heredity, father, real estate, childhood, emotions.

HOUSE 5: Love, pleasure, recreation, children, creation, luck with games, relationships with children.

HOUSE 6: Everyday life, daily work, colleagues, subordinates, health.

UN-CONSCIOUS:

HOUSE 7: DESCENDANT: Unions, marriage, the other, associations, contracts, the subject's attitude toward others, spouse, partners.

HOUSE 8: Passions, crises, transformations, the subject's real or symbolic death, investments, sexuality, birth, inheritance, other people's money, secrets, occult science.

HOUSE 9: Big trips, spirituality, the foreign, philosophy, higher education scholars, the abstract, rights and legalities.

HOUSE 10: MIDHEAVEN: Social success, professional destiny, mother, career, ambitions, the public, celebrity, the highest potential of the subject.

HOUSE 11: Friends, group projects, support and protection, humanitarian life, relationship with people and the world, aspirations.

HOUSE 12: Enemies, trouble, loneliness, hidden difficulties, secrets, the inner Self, serious illness, hospitals, prisons, convents, any place of confinement, inner crises, the un-*conscious*, the family un-*conscious*, the family shadow.

▽ △ For the majority of the Universal Laws △▽:

Inspired by the Laws in the following book: COUPAL, Marie. *Le Guide Du Rêve et de Ses Symboles.* De A À Z, tous les sens de vos rêves, Paris, Éditions J'AI LU, 2008.

Chapter 1: "Law of the Will" « Loi de la Volonté »

Chapter 2: "Law of Attraction" « Loi de l'Attraction »

Chapter 3: "Law of Vibration" « Loi de la Vibration »

Chapter 4: "Law of Realization" « Loi de la Réalisation »

Chapter 5: "Law of Inspiration" « Loi d'Inspiration »

Chapter 6: "Law of Free Choice in Love" « Loi du Libre Choix en Amour »

Chapter 7: "Law of Responsibility" « Loi des Responsabilités »

Chapter 8: "Law of Cause and Effect" and "Law of Consequences" « Loi de Cause à Effet »

Chapter 9: "Law of *Know*ledge" « Loi de Connaissance »

Chapter 10: "Law of Cycles" « Loi des Cycles »

Chapter 11: "Law of Absolute Effort" « Loi de l'Effort Absolu »

Chapter 12: "Law of Compensation" « Loi de Compensation »

Chapter 13: "Law of Transformation" « Loi des Transformations »

Chapter 14: "Law of Transformation by the purification of what is dark in the Un-*Conscious*" « Loi de Transformation par le nettoyage de tout ce qui est obscur dans l'inconscient »

Chapter 15: "Law of Diabolic Forces" « Loi des Forces Diaboliques, intérêt exagéré pour le Matériel »

Chapter 16: "Law of the Balance of Opposites" « Loi de l'Équilibre des Opposés »

Chapter 17: "Law of Life Moderations" « Loi de l'Économie de Vie »

Chapter 18: "Law of Rhythm" « Loi du Rythme »

Chapter 19: "Law of Polarity" « Loi de Polarité »

Chapter 20: "Law of Reincarnation" « Loi de Réincarnation »

Chapter 21: "Law of Correspondence" « Loi de Correspondances »

▽ △ Some details about the chakras, positions, colours … △▽:

Inspired by the following book: WOLF, Élias. *Le Livre des 28 Chakras,* Les principaux centres d'énergie de notre corps, Paris, Guy Trédaniel Éditeur, 2007.

Chapter	Chakra	Position	Primary Colour / Complementary Colour
1	Root or base (primary chakra)	At the level of the perineum, between the anus and genitals ; downward	Bright red/ Cyan
2	sacral (primary chakra)	Midway between the navel and the pubic bone	Orange/ Light blue
3	Solar Plexus (primary chakra)	Center body, above the sternum	Canary yellow/ Dark blue
4	heart (primary chakra)	Middle of chest, breast height	Emerald green/ Magenta
5	throat (primary chakra)	Throat, larynx height	Royal blue/ Sun yellow
6	third eye or brow (primary chakra)	between the eyes at the bridge of the nose	Indigo/ Yellow green
7	crown (primary chakra)	At the top of the head, pointing upwards	Purple/ Neon green
8	hara (other body chakra)	Near the spine at the level of the navel (up to 2 finger widths above or below)	Orange-yellow/ Medium blue
9	kalpa taru (other body chakra)	Halfway between the third and the fourth chakras (solar plexus and heart chakras)	Grass green/ Lilac
10	thymus (other body chakra)	In the middle of the chest, midway between the heart and the throat chakra	Turquoise/ Ruby

Chapter	Chakra	Position	Primary Colour / Complementary Colour
11	Back of the head chakra (other body chakra)	In the middle of the back of the head two or three finger widths above the third eye	Glacier blue/ Nut brown
12	The upper forehead chakra (other body chakra)	On the forehead, midway between the third eye and the crown chakra	Purple blue/ light green
13	Feet chakra (body points)	Toward the middle of the foot downward	Bright red/ Cyan (like root chakra)
14	Knee chakra (body points)	At the level of the knees, radiates in a double cone shape	Orange/ Light blue(like sacral chakra)
15	Elbow chakra (body points)	At the level of the elbows, radiates in a double cone shape (like knee chakras)	Canary yellow/ Dark blue (like solar plexus chakra)
16	Hand chakra (body points)	At the center of the palms	Emerald green/Magenta(like heart chakra)
17	Soul chakra (supra personal chakras)	A hand's breadth above the crown chakra	Saturated dark steel blue/Olive green
18	Gate of the Soul (supra personal chakras)	40 to 50 cm above the head	Medium blue Lilac /dark avocado green(both via interpolation)
19	The Superior guidance gate (supra personal chakras)	Above the head, wrist height when the arms are stretched upwards	Azure blue/Golden Olive

Chapter	Chakra	Position	Primary Colour / Complementary Colour
20	The vocation center (supra personal chakras)	Above the head, at the tips of the fingers, when the arms are extended upward	Azure dark blue/Light golden Olive
21	The Celestial Star (supra personal chakras)	At about two arm lengths (to the ends of the fingers), or 2 meters above the head	Dark purple blue/Gold

▽ △ Inspiration taken from the following statements △▽:

Inspired by the following book: GUIN, Catherine. *Le Tarot, mon miroir.* Avec le Tarot, de lame en lame, je m'ouvre, je grandis en conscience et je chemine vers QUI JE SUIS, Québec, Les Éditions ATMA internationales, 2010.

Chapter 1: "I can do All!" « Je peux tout ! »

Chapter 2: "I know everything!" « Je sais tout ! »

Chapter 3: "I create and communicate.". « Je crée et communique. »

Chapter 4: "I take responsibility for what I have created." « J'assume ma responsabilité de ce qui a été créé. »

Chapter 5: "I know, and I will teach you if you want." « Je sais, alors je vais t'enseigner si tu veux. »

Chapter 6: "I choose myself before anything else." « Je me choisis avant toute chose. »

Chapter 7: "I am going forward on my life path."« J'avance sur le chemin de ma vie. »

Chapter 8: "Whatever happens is *All* right." « Quoiqu'il arrive tout est juste. »

Chapter 9: "I take the time to stop and think." « Je prends le temps de faire le point. »

Chapter 10: "I become the centered observer." « Je deviens l'observateur centré. »

Chapter 11: "I am the master of my emotions and I express them calmly." « Je suis maître de mes émotions et les exprime calmement. »

Chapter 12: "I trust that everything that happens to me is for the best." « J'ai confiance, il m'arrive le meilleur. »

Chapter 13: "I agree to die in the old way." « J'accepte de mourir à l'ancien. »

Chapter 14: "I let go and receive *All* solutions." « Je lâche-prise et reçois toutes les solutions. »

Chapter 15: "I enjoy freely what I have." « Je jouis en liberté de ce que j'ai. »

Chapter 16: "I open myself up to my Superior *consciousness*." « Je m'ouvre à ma conscience Supérieure. »

Chapter 17: "I work with my intuition." « J'œuvre avec mon intuition. »

Chapter 18: "I exist. I am unique. I make myself clear." « J'existe. Je suis unique. Je me clarifie. »

Chapter 19: "I marvel at myself and I enjoy my life." « Je m'émerveille et je suis la joie de vivre. »

Chapter 20: "I am new with every moment." « Je suis nouveau à chaque instant. »

Chapter 21: "I self realize. I succeed at everything I do." « Je me réalise. Je réussis tout ce que j'entreprends. »

Chapter 0 or 22: "I have a strong faith that keeps me going." « J'ai une foi inébranlable qui me permet de continuer. »

▽ △ Opening the sacred space△ ▽:

VILLOLDO, Alberto. *Shaman, Healer, Sage.* How to heal yourself and others with the energy medicine of the Americas, New York, Published by Harmony Books, 2000.

Invocation

"To the winds of the South
Great serpent,
Wrap your coils of light around us,
Teach us to shed the past the way you shed your skin,
To walk softly on the Earth.
Teach us the Beauty Way.

To the winds of the West
Mother jaguar,
Protect our medicine space.
Teach us the way of peace, to live impeccably
Show us the way beyond death.

To the winds of the North.
Hummingbird, Grandmothers and Grandfathers,
Ancient Ones
Come and warm your hands by our fires
Whisper to us in the wind
We honor you who have come before us,

And you who will come after us, our children's children.

To the winds of the East.
Great eagle, condor
Come to us from the place of the rising Sun.
Keep us under your wing.
Show us the mountains we only dare to dream of.
Teach us to fly wing to wing with the Great Spirit.

Mother Earth.
We've gathered for the healing of all your children.
The Stone People, the Plant People.
The four-legged, the two-legged, the creepy crawlers.
The finned, the furred, and the winged ones.
All our relations.

Father Sun, Grandmother Moon, to the Star Nations.
Great Spirit, you who are known by a thousand names
And you who are the unnamable One.
Thank you for bringing us together
And allowing us to sing the Song of Life."

PRAYER FOR CREATING SACRED SPACE

▽ △▽ △▽ △▽ △▽ △▽ △▽ △

Bibliography

.•° .•° .•° .•°.

CHEVALIER, Jean et GHEERBRANT, Alain. *Dictionnaire Des Symboles*. Mythes, rêves, coutumes, gestes, formes, figures, couleurs, nombres, Paris, Éditions Robert Laffont, S.A. et Éditions Jupiter, 2005.

CHEVALIER, Jean et GHEERBRANT, Alain. *Dictionary of Symbols*. Great Britain, Blackwell Publishers, Penguin Reference, 1994. Translated by Buchanan-Brown.

COUPAL, Marie. *Le Guide Du Rêve et de Ses Symboles*. De A À Z, tous les sens de vos rêves, Paris, Éditions J'AI LU, 2008.

DYER, Wayne. *Entrer au cœur du silence*. Prendre consciemment contact avec Dieu grâce à la méditation, Varennes, Éditions ADA inc., 2006. Traduit de l'américain par Christian Hallé.

FERRINI, Paul. *Les Douze Étapes Du Pardon*. Manuel pratique pour passer de la peur à l'amour, Varennes, Éditions ADA inc., 2010. Traduit de l'anglais par Sylvie Mayrand.

FERRINI, Paul. *The 12 steps of Forgiveness*. A practical Manual for moving from fear to Love, Greenfield MA, Heartways Press, 1991.

BOSCHIERO, Reynald Georges. *Dictionnaire de la Lithothérapie*. Propriétés énergétiques des pierres et cristaux naturels, Genève 3, Suisse, Editions AMBRE, 2005.

GUIN, Catherine. *Le Tarot, mon miroir*. Avec le Tarot, de lame en lame, je m'ouvre, je grandis en conscience et je chemine vers

QUI JE SUIS, Québec, Les Éditions ATMA internationales, 2010.

LABONTÉ, Marie Lise. *Les Familles D'Âmes,* d'après les enseignements des anges Xedah et de l'archange Michaël, Loretteville, Éditions Le Dauphin Blanc, 2002.

MILLMAN, Dan. *Votre Chemin de Vie.* Une méthode pour en découvrir le but, Éditions du Roseau, 1995. Traduit de l'anglais par Denis Ouellet.

MILLMAN, Dan. *The Life you were born to live.* A guide to finding your life purpose, AN H J Kramer book, 1993.

MYSS, Caroline. *Contrats Sacrés.* Éveiller votre potentiel divin, Varennes, Éditions ADA inc., 2002, 2003.

MYSS, Caroline. Sacred Contracts. Awakening your divine potential, Three rivers Press, 2002, 2003.

PROPHET, CLARE, Élisabeth. *La Flamme Violette.* Pour guérir le corps, l'esprit et l'âme, Montréal, Les Éditions Lumière d'El Morya, 2006.

SHINN SCOVEL, Florence. *Le Jeu de la Vie.* Paris, Éditions E Bussière Astra, 1941. Traduit de l'anglais par Dr. Mary Sterling.

SHINN SCOVEL, Florence. *The game of Life.* Winning rules for success & happiness, Vermilion, 1925.

Un Cours en Miracles, Éditions du Roseau, 2005. Traduit de l'anglais par Denis Ouellet en collaboration avec Franchita Cattani.

A Course in Miracles, Foundation for inner peace, combined volume (third edition), 2007.

VILLOLDO, Alberto. *Chaman Des Temps Modernes.* L'art de la guérison par la médecine énergétique des autochtones d'Amérique, Varennes, Éditions ADA inc., 2007.

VILLOLDO, Alberto. *Shaman, Healer, Sage.* How to heal yourself and others with the energy medicine of the Americas, New York, Harmony Books, 2000.

VIRTUE, Doreen. *Archanges et Maîtres Ascensionnés.* Comment travailler et guérir avec les divinités et les déités, Varennes, Éditions ADA inc., 2004. Adapté de l'anglais par Lou Lamontagne.

VIRTUE, Doreen. *Archangels & Ascended Masters.* A guide to working and healing with Divinities and Deities, Hay House, 2003.

VIRTUE, Doreen. *La Voie Des Artisans De Lumière.* Réveillez votre pouvoir spirituel de la connaissance et de la guérison, Varennes, Éditions ADA inc., 2007. Traduit de l'américain par Lou Lamontagne.

VIRTUE, Doreen. *The Light Worker's Way.* Awakening your spiritual power to know and heal, Hay House, 1997.

WOLF, Élias. *Le Livre des 28 Chakras.* Les principaux centres d'énergie de notre corps, Paris, Guy Trédaniel Éditeur, 2007.

I would like to thank *All* the authors for creating and sharing such valuable growth tools... Tools that have contributed, among other things, to the birth of: Chant-All the Alchemist Fairy returning to the Source of *All* and much more, since any tool that helps spiritual growth eventually contributes, one way or another, to en*light*enment!

A thousand thanks - Creators!!!

About the Author

☆Chantal Leduc☆ is a Writer, Author, Editor, Professional certified NLP Coach, Coach in Energy Communication, Spiritual Teacher, Soul *Awakener*, Channel and Healer. She is also the owner of "Coaching Claire Vision Chantou" and "Les Éditions Chantou" and much more! She is an eternal student who Loves to share her *know*ledge, hence the interest in writing books, giving entertaining workshops and speeches. She channels her *know*ledge in the best interest of the receivers for the present moment. Here is the first book "Chant-*All* the Alchemist Fairy returning to the Source of *All*"... of a trilogy. Two more books will follow... because there is still a lot of information to come.

One of the main goals of this book is to use it in workshops either one on one or in groups. I currently teach tarot utilizing it as a reference tool. I created a 23 week course based on a week per major Arcanum (there are 22 major Arcana) and an extra week to finalize the course. Each week you receive a PDF document by email for the course and the week after, we meet, in person, by phone or via Skype. That way you receive one hour per week of Coaching with me. The course consists of a theoretical and a practical part with the practical part being 99.999% of the course. I consider this course to be a powerful tool for helping you familiarize yourSelf with the different energy of each Arcanum. It will help you hear the voice of your own intuition and enable you to interpret your own symbols and signs and much more! At the end you will be able to do Soul readings... for yourSelf and others and you will also be able to recognize the energy of each Arcanum... energy that corresponds to different archetypes or masks. This course is one of the courses that has transformed my whole existence so that I am now able to Guide you during your own Life transformation!

Are you good at organizing groups or would you like to participate in a workshop with a friend? I offer a 10% discount off the price of the course per person referred. Contact me at 450 544-1375 or chantal@coachingchantou.com it will be a pleasure to meet you!

Follow me on my weekly online radio show on Wednesdays at 11 a.m.in French or at 4 p.m. in English live or at your convenience, the link is good for 30 days after the show and you can also download it and listen to it later. Find the link on my facebook page or write me an email requesting my weekly newsletter which has the link to my show.

Note: The information regarding any type of promotion may vary without notice. We reserve the right to make changes at any time.